*f*P

MY HOPE FOR
PEACE

JEHAN SADAT

FREE PRESS

New York   London   Toronto   Sydney

FREE PRESS
A Division of Simon & Schuster, Inc.
1230 Avenue of the Americas
New York, NY 10020

First Free Press hardcover edition March 2009

FREE PRESS and colophon are
trademarks of Simon & Schuster, Inc.

For information about special discounts for bulk purchases,
please contact Simon & Schuster Special Sales at
1-800-456-6798 or business@simonandschuster.com

The Simon & Schuster Speakers Bureau can bring authors to
your live event. For more information or to book an event contact
the Simon & Schuster Speakers Bureau at 866-248-3049 or
visit our website at www.simonspeakers.com

Designed by Kyoko Watanabe
Maps by Paul J. Pugliese

Manufactured in the United States of America

10   9   8   7   6   5   4   3   2   1

Library of Congress Cataloging-in-Publication Data
Sadat, Jehan.
My hope for peace / Jehan Sadat.
p. cm.
Includes bibliographical references and index.
1. Arab-Israeli conflict—1993—Peace. 2. September 11 Terrorist Attacks, 2001—
Influence. 3. Islam and politics—Arab countries. 4. Sadat, Anwar, 1918–1981—
Assassination. I. Title.
DS79.76.S22 2009
956.05'3—dc22   2008032100

ISBN-13: 978-1-4165-9221-1

For my family, for peace,
in memory of my husband—Anwar Sadat

Weapons alone are easy for all men to have, yet claws alone do not make a lion brave.

—al Mutanabbi

Contents

MY HOPE FOR
PEACE

Introduction

*P*EACE. THIS WORD, THIS IDEA—THIS GOAL—IS THE DEFINING theme of my life.

First, and perhaps most obvious, I refer to the ongoing struggle for peace in the Middle East: a just, comprehensive settlement between Arabs and Israelis, one that will help to eliminate at least one source of hatred, extremism, and misery in the world; one that will allow the inhabitants of these most holy places to live side by side, amicably, securely, productively. This is the cause for which my husband, Anwar Sadat, gave his life. On October 6, 1981, he was assassinated by Islamic fanatics who believed that the peace he forged with Israel would perish along with him. They were wrong. The 1979 Egyptian-Israeli treaty, signed as a direct result of the Camp David Accords of 1978, has endured some thirty years, a reminder of the fact that seemingly insuperable rifts can be bridged and a foundation for a just resolution can be constructed. In one of his last interviews, my husband was asked what three wishes he would like to see fulfilled in his lifetime. He answered, "One, peace in the Middle East. Two, peace in the Middle East. Three, peace in the Middle East." For him, this dream is finished. His dream is now mine.

Since 1985, I have been lecturing, teaching, and fund-raising to further that dream. Living in both my native Cairo and in a suburb of Washington, D.C., and being a professor, a peace activist, a former first lady, and a private citizen, I have had a front-row seat to the agonizing cycle of progress and setback in the Middle East and noted how my husband's ideas, once unilaterally rejected by the Arab world, have come to be widely accepted. Now, with the thirtieth anniversary of his historic trip to Jerusalem just behind us and the urgent need for a new paradigm all too plainly before us, it's high time we reexamine his legacy.

In addition to the end of conflict between Arabs and Israelis, *My Hope for Peace* refers to the peace inherent in Islam. I am not the first to point out that in Arabic, the word for peace, *Salam*, and *Islam* share the same etymological root, the same essence. Most Muslims understand and—figuratively speaking—strive to live this relationship. Sadly, for most non-Muslims, the link is lost in translation. Instead, in the post-9/11 world, Islam is generally regarded with suspicion or outright hostility as a faith of violent fanatics. In some ways, I can understand this, for I have felt the effects of such fanaticism firsthand. And yet because I have come face-to-face with extremism, I can say categorically that it is not Islam. As a lifelong Muslim, someone who has found in her faith a source of sustenance and right counsel, this is a distinction that is perhaps easier for me to make. I see and hear these supposedly missing "moderate Muslims" every day. Similarly, by virtue of my lecturing, teaching, and residing in the United States, it is clear that while there is much media coverage devoted to Muslim misdeeds, there is a dearth of actual knowledge about my faith. When countered with images of angry men waving Qur'ans and burning American flags, women draped head to toe in burkas, and dark rumblings about "Islamo-fascism," the oft-mouthed words "Islam is a religion of peace" lose their efficacy. Moreover, there is a general belief that in addition to the actual conflicts that plague the planet, we are engaged in something of a meta-war, the so-called clash of civilizations, which pits Islam against the West in a battle for world dominion. Accurate? Absolutely not. Self-fulfilling? Quite possibly.

Although I am not a religious scholar, I hope to set the record straight and correct what I see as the most persistent and prevalent misconceptions about Islam—among them, that it is a monolithic movement, bent on overturning the rule of law, subjugating women, and forcibly converting infidels; that Islam is inherently violent, a religion of fanatics that sanctions any atrocity in the name of jihad; and that Muslims hate "freedom" and are incapable, by nature and belief, of democracy. I also call on my own experience as a believer to illustrate my points, for Islam, like all other faiths, cannot be understood only as a collection of beliefs, but as it transforms and inspires the lives of the individuals who follow it.

The third and final way in which the theme of peace manifests in my life has been wholly personal—a search, if you will, for inner peace. As a consequence of 9/11—a day that, for reasons I set out in the next chapter, unleashed a torrent of memory—I have found myself trying to evaluate my own life. There is, of course, no shortage of outside opinions on which I can draw; I have been both praised and excoriated for being a "feminist," hailed as a pioneer for women's rights in the Arab world and deplored as a destroyer of families, accused of being a mere mouthpiece for my husband and also an undue influence on him. For better and for worse, I have been a polarizing figure, primarily for my ideas about and work on behalf of women and the family. In the wake of my husband's death, however, all my "progressive" ideals were put to the test. Time and time again, I had urged Egyptian women to establish a sense of an independent self; thus, I could not retreat into Anwar's shadow. I had to stand on my own two feet. Although I might have remained in Egypt, living the rest of my life in the bosom of my family, I felt I had to establish an identity for myself. I moved to the United States, finished my doctorate, and began teaching and lecturing. Bolstering me was the proud legacy of Egyptian feminism, to which I have long turned for inspiration, my family, and my faith, which has ever exhorted women to education and equality. Indeed, I see myself as part of a tradition of strong Muslim, Arab, and Egyptian women, not an anomaly or a sellout to the West. Drawing on my varied professional experiences—as a political wife, a first lady, an advocate for peace and women's rights, and an academic—as well as my experience as a wife and mother in a society that is both traditional and devout, I feel that I am well qualified to dispel a few of the old myths about Oriental women that have found new life. We are not all benighted and oppressed, subservient or terrorized. And while there are enormous obstacles for women in the Muslim world, the roadblock is not Islam. While I cannot answer for all Muslims, I can say that Islam does not hate women, but rather enjoins us to claim our God-given equality.

Just as the theme of peace that permeates this book is threefold, it seems to me that waging peace happens on three fronts. The first is through the good offices of governments and international organizations as they negotiate treaties, hammer out compromises, and craft carefully worded statements. This work is as difficult as it is essential, and from past diplomatic efforts, including my husband's initiatives, we can draw crucial lessons for the future. The second takes place on an interpersonal level, in our behaviors and actions toward our presumptive enemies. In such a context, we all—Israelis and Arabs, Muslims and Westerners—are called to be wise, skillful, and visionary. And with these in short supply, we cannot afford to sit back and hope that presidents and policy experts can solve our problems for us. Treaties alone cannot overcome generations of animosity—but grassroots action can.

And the third space in which we must wage peace? It is, of course, within ourselves—in our intention. Muslims call this *niyya*. In Islam, it is not just our deeds that are important, but also the contents of our hearts when we undertake them. Indeed, there is a famous saying of the Prophet that "all actions are judged by motives, and each person will be rewarded according to his intention." Peace is always treated as such an impossible goal, a utopian dream, but if regular people can cultivate the intention of peace—toward ourselves, toward the planet on which we live and the people with whom we share it—then *insha'allah*, God willing, we can achieve it.

Eleventh of September,
Sixth of October

Wᴴᴱɴ ᴛᴇʀʀᴏʀɪsᴛs ᴀᴛᴛᴀᴄᴋᴇᴅ ᴛʜᴇ Uɴɪᴛᴇᴅ Sᴛᴀᴛᴇs ᴏɴ Sᴇᴘ-tember 11, 2001, I was in my home in northern Virginia, having returned from Egypt only a few days before. I had slept late that Tuesday morning, still jet-lagged from my travels, and switched on CNN. My plans were modest, and in keeping with years of habit, I would sort through the mail that had accumulated in my absence, make a trip to the grocery store to pick up a few supplies, and slowly readjust to the rhythms of my American schedule. The flashing red alert that scrolled across the television screen, however, signaled that this was not to be a day engaged in comforting routine. Like so many other people across the country, and indeed, around the world, I could not believe what had taken place and what was taking place before my eyes: people trapped and dying in the twin towers, a section of the Pentagon smoldering, and later, in the fields of Pennsylvania, a fourth plane crashing to the earth, killing all on board.

As the horror unfolded, the enormity of it all sank in. Militant fundamentalists purporting to be Muslims had perpetrated an unthinkable crime. The twin towers had fallen, the rescue efforts had ended before they were begun, the number of dead was still uncertain. Like every other resident of the United States, I was in a state of profound shock. And yet, scarcely believable as the flickering images on the television seemed to me—to everyone—I remembered another autumn day in which zealots had shattered lives, sown confusion, and plunged a nation into turmoil: October 6, 1981. The day my husband, Anwar Sadat, the president of Egypt, was assassinated.

He was killed because he had done the unimaginable, and for some angry few, the unforgivable: he had negotiated peace with Israel. It was his life's work, and indeed he gave his life for it. Radical Islamists branded him a traitor, a *kafir*, or unbeliever, and an apostate, and on a brilliant, blue-skied day that gave no presentiment of the horror to come, he was gunned down in full view of his family, his nation, and the world.

On that awful Tuesday in 2001, I could not help but remember. The events of his death are seared into my memory. I was seated in the stands as Anwar reviewed the military parade that commemorated his 1973 victory over Israel. Suddenly a truck stopped in front of the stand where my husband, along with Vice President Hosni Mubarak, other members of the government, and international dignitaries, were seated. Three men hurled grenades and fired into the crowd, and a fourth burst forth from the truck, spraying the stand with machine-gun fire. Anwar was standing at attention when the bullets struck him.

My husband had been fatally wounded.

I was in shock, and soon after, Egypt was reeling. In those first terrible hours, there was so much uncertainty. We did not know whether the assassination was the work of a few individuals or the beginning of something bigger—a coup d'état, a revolution like the one that had ushered in the Ayatollah Khomeini in Iran not many years before. It was a feeling I never thought I would experience again, but in the first hours following the September 11 attacks, when it was unclear whether more violence was imminent, how widespread the plot was, or who had executed it, I was overcome with déjà vu.

The situations were, of course, different in a million substantial ways, but the dread, confusion, and shock of living through a national crisis and a human tragedy—these feelings assaulted me with a terrible familiarity. I felt I had some idea of what must be happening in the government: the emergency meetings, the furious scramble for information, the pressure to maintain calm, the pressure to act. I even recognized the measured, reassuring tone of the government spokespeople, a tone that only partially concealed their underlying bewilderment. I had used it myself twenty years before.

One by one, each of my four grown children called me from overseas, begging me to come home to Cairo. I did not believe myself to be in any danger, but my proximity to Washington, D.C., a likely target for further attacks, made my children uneasy. I had little desire to flee the United States, but—my children must have realized—I could not have made the trip even if I wanted to. They too had experienced the turmoil following the terrorist attack on their father, and they must have realized, as I did, that all travel in and out of the country would be halted. I was slated to do a speaking engagement in Reno, Nevada. Much as I love my work as a lecturer, I was relieved that for the time being, getting to Reno was impossible. The organizer phoned me repeatedly, anxious to ascertain that I was still coming. Politely, I put her off; we needed to await official word from the government before trying to resume our daily life. How could I give a lecture during a national crisis? In the days that followed, I wondered who would care about the legacy of Anwar Sadat, of peace, when it seemed that the nation was girding for war—even though it was not yet clear where and at whom America could strike.

I spent the hours and days that followed glued to the TV. And as more details emerged on the perpetrators of the attacks, it became increasingly obvious that my sense of the connection between September 11, 2001 and October 6, 1981 was not limited to my own, now nauseating sense of déjà vu. Both attacks had been perpetrated by Muslim fanatics, people who dreamed of overthrowing the existing order and replacing it with a "pure" Islamic state. People who twisted the tenets of my faith and the faith of million of others to commit atrocities under the banner of Islam. My heart broke for the families of the victims, for I felt I had some insight into their sudden, shocking loss, which was at once intensely private and excruciatingly public. I knew they were entering into a nightmare from which they would not soon, or perhaps ever, truly emerge. Some twenty-six years after Anwar's life was so brutally ended, I still acutely feel his absence. He was my husband of more than thirty-two years, my solace, my friend, the love of my life.

In addition to sadness, I was also filled with fear—not for myself but for Islam, and all Muslims who revile the crimes that have been committed in a so-called holy war in which they want no part. I suspected that this day would have repercussions for Muslims in every part of the world. And of course, my heart sank when I found out that Egyptians were among the 9/11 conspirators. But it nearly stopped when I heard the name Ayman Zawahiri. I could not believe my ears: this man had been implicated in the plot against my husband. He was indeed a killer, and my country had sought to bring him to justice for many years. Zawahiri was a physician; it is a bitter irony that a man who is morally bound to protect life should prove to be a mass murderer. He grew up in a middle-class neighborhood in Cairo and came from a respectable Egyptian family, belying the idea that extremism is always a product of poverty or lack of opportunity. Although not one of the men who actually attacked my husband, he was deeply involved in al-Jihad, one of the terrorist organizations plotting to overthrow Sadat's government. Zawahiri was arrested after Sadat's assassination, tried, and found guilty of dealing in weapons. He served a three-year sentence and then fled to Saudi Arabia, where he eventually joined forces with Osama bin Laden.

Zawahiri, however, resurfaced in Egypt long before September 11. In the 1990s, he was involved in a series of terrible attacks within my country, employing a grisly weapon that had, until then, been unheard of by even the most extreme Sunni Muslim group: the suicide bomber. Suicide, like murder, is strictly forbidden in Islam, but again, the zealots had perverted the Qur'an to justify their actions. On the eighteenth anniversary of my husband's historic trip to Jerusalem, a trip that was the bold first step to establish peace between Israel and Egypt, Zawahiri used suicide bombers to destroy the Egyptian embassy in Islamabad. Sixteen innocent people were killed, and many, many more were injured. Suicide bombers would become a hallmark of al-Jihad and later, as the world now knows, al Qaeda.

Zawahiri's murderous campaign in Egypt reached its peak with the 1997 attacks on Luxor, the ancient pharaonic city situated on the banks of the Nile. Even as the primary Islamist organization within Egypt, the Muslim Brotherhood, forswore violence, a promise that it has held to this day, Zawahiri and al-Jihad joined with factions of the Islamic Group, to carry out an attack in the magnificent funerary Temple of Queen Hatshepsut in Luxor, where sixty-two people, fifty-six of them tourists, were slain in cold blood. It was the worst terrorist incident in Egypt's history.

The terrorists had hoped to cripple the nation by attacking tourism, a mainstay of Egypt's economy, and indeed, the tourism industry was dealt a terrible blow. People by the thousands cancelled their trips, frightened by the gruesome violence. But the tactic backfired, and the Egyptian people, who felt the losses keenly, were incensed. Moreover, they were sickened by the violence. Any vestige of sympathy the people might have had for the fanatics vanished: it was all too clear that their bloody vision of Islam was not shared by the citizens of Egypt. Interestingly, from his cell in a United States prison, the spiritual leader of the Islamic Group perhaps realized the miscalculation and attempted to disown the action. His name has also become familiar to American readers: Sheikh Omar Abdel Rahman.

Like Ayman Zawahiri, his was a name I had never expected to hear again, and certainly not in the United States. Abdel Rahman is now serving a life sentence for his role in the 1993 World Trade Center bombing. The so-called blind sheikh had also been implicated in the death of my husband. Abdel Rahman had issued the *fatwah*, or religious ruling, stating that the faithful have the right to kill a heretical leader. And since the radical fundamentalists—a vocal, violent minority—were calling peace with Israel a heresy, it was an obvious invitation to assassination. Because Abdel Rahman did not mention Sadat by name, he served only a brief sentence and was expelled from the country. Shockingly, despite his well-known connections to my husband's murderers—he was on the United States State Department's list of known terrorists—he was granted legal entry to the United States. He settled in Jersey City, New Jersey, just across the river from his eventual targets, where he preached his message of violence and hatred with absolute impunity. He even traveled across the United States and Canada, fund-raising to support his murderous schemes. Under his guidance, his followers plotted widespread attacks against well-known civilian targets in the New York metropolitan area. I still cannot understand why, in the wake of the first World Trade Center bombing, Rahman was not returned to Egypt to stand trial. Instead, he is comfortably lodged in an American prison, where he still occasionally manages to broadcast his hateful directives.

As is painfully apparent from the preceding paragraphs, the struggle against terrorism is not new to Egypt. We have been fighting it for decades. For literally thousands of years, Egypt has been a civilized, cosmopolitan nation, whose people have reviled violence and welcomed peace. People of many faiths have lived side by side for centuries, and violent fundamentalism runs contrary to the moderate Egyptian character. It is true, however, that the modern roots of political Islam (which is *not* synonymous with terrorism) are bound up with the recent history of my country. And since our lives, for better and worse, are also linked to this history, a brief lesson is in order.

Most experts agree that the modern idea of political Islam was advanced by Hassan al-Banna, who founded the Muslim Brotherhood in Egypt in 1928, four years after the Ottoman caliphate was abolished. He saw in Islam not only a religion but also a viable system encompassing all aspects of life; thus, he and his followers sought to create an Islamic state, governed completely by Qur'anic law. At the time, Egypt was a monarchy, ruled by the descendants of the erstwhile Ottoman governor, Mohammed Ali Pasha (himself Albanian), but it was the British who were truly in charge. The protectorate had been established in 1882, when British troops arrived to guard their investment in the Suez Canal, something they regarded as key to maintaining control over their empire in India; and the British were *still* there, a thorn in the side of Egyptian patriots, when al-Banna founded his Brotherhood.

Al-Banna's organization resonated with many Egyptians, who saw in the Brotherhood a political system that acknowledged their deep faith, was not imposed by a foreign power, and was genuinely and actively engaged in providing the people with much-needed social services. By the time I was a girl in Cairo, the Brotherhood, in stark contrast to the corrupt rule of the dissolute King Farouk or the self-interested colonial administration of the British, offered ordinary Egyptians free medical clinics and schooling. Its membership grew exponentially, spreading to neighborhoods and villages all over Egypt and, later, the Muslim world.

The Brotherhood was not solely philanthropic, however. It also had a "secret apparatus," or military wing, and in the late 1940s it launched terrorist attacks against the government, the British, and the foreign communities within Egypt. King Farouk's government outlawed the Brotherhood, and Brotherhood members responded by killing the prime minister; two months later, the government responded by having al-Banna himself gunned down in the street. Egyptians witnessed these developments with deep uneasiness. Although both Anwar and I were vehemently opposed to British colonial rule and wanted the British out of Egypt, neither he nor I thought the secret armed wing of the Muslim Brotherhood could accomplish this goal. It was clear that such a cycle of violence and reprisal was not in Egypt's best interests. I agreed with Anwar, who had risen through the ranks of the army, that change should come from within the legitimate institution of the Egyptian military.

Three years later, it did. In 1952, the Free Officers Coup—in which my husband of three years was a key player—ousted the British. This group of nine young Egyptian officers also forced the king to abdicate, and for the first time in thousands of years placed Egyptians in charge of their own nation. And the fact that all of this was achieved without bloodshed makes it all the more extraordinary. Much to the dismay of the Brotherhood, the Free Officers had no interest in ushering in a theocracy. Al-Banna's followers found themselves increasingly at odds with the new order, and in 1954, the Brotherhood tried to take over the fledgling government, were stopped, once again disbanded, and, as would become a pattern, went underground. Later that same year, they nearly succeeded in assassinating President Nasser. In the wake of that very near miss, thousands of people with ties to the Brotherhood were called in for questioning, and many were arrested. My husband, who had been recently appointed minister of state, served as one of three judges on the court that was convened to try them. Anwar immediately began receiving death threats, establishing a sad norm for much of our public life.

One of those imprisoned after the attempt on Nasser's life was a man named Sayyed Qutb, who, in the power vacuum left by al-Banna's assassination, had become an influential leader in the Muslim Brotherhood. A schoolteacher and civil servant, he had spent two years studying in the United States, where he was disgusted by what he saw as the licentiousness of the West. He returned to Egypt, convinced that the United States capitalist system was morally bankrupt, and he went on to be a powerful ideologue for the Muslim Brotherhood. In prison, he became increasingly radicalized. In his book *Milestones,* written in jail and published during his brief release from prison in 1964, he declared that all countries, including Muslim ones, existed in a state of *jahilliya*—pre-Islamic barbarism and ignorance. Traditionally, Islam has used this word to refer to the condition of the Arabs in the time before Mohammed. Qutb, however, used it to describe the contemporary world. He believed that the only acceptable government was one that cleaved to his strict, fundamentalist vision of Islam and encouraged Muslims to move against any state that deviated from this ideal. This paved the way for radicals to "excommunicate" fellow Muslims. The practice of declaring a Muslim an unbeliever, or *kafir*, is known as *takfir*. *Takfir* has become a convenient means for terrorists to kill with impunity and still believe, despite all the blood on their hands, that they are headed for paradise. *Milestones* has provided ideological inspiration for many radical Islamists, including Sheikh Omar Abdel Rahman, Ayman Zawahiri, and Osama bin Laden.

These subjects are quite difficult for me write about, given the heartbreaking way in which the repercussions of such philosophizing would manifest in my own life. Qutb was tried for his role in the attempted assassination, found guilty, and, in 1966, sentenced to death by Nasser. Nasser, however, offered to commute his sentence to life in prison if he would disown the tactics he put forth in *Milestones*. Anwar himself was sent as an envoy to offer Qutb the deal. The man refused, convinced that if he died a martyr, his ideas would go on to have greater influence: the spread of Islamic radicalism.

Islamic fundamentalism would gain much ground in the wake of the disastrous 1967 war with Israel, known in America as the Six-Day War. This was deeply humiliating to the Arab nations, which had seen our armies defeated in one blow; the Egyptian air force had been destroyed before it left the ground. As an eyewitness to these events, I find it impossible to overstate the impact of this loss in terms of lives and property, as well as political stature. The Arab nations lost control of the Sinai, the West Bank, the Golan Heights, the Gaza Strip, and Jerusalem.

In the wake of that bitter loss, psychological and territorial, a new religiosity took hold. Some people believed that our defeat was a sign of God's disfavor—that we had lost our way spiritually and were being punished. What we needed to do, they argued, was to return to the faith as it was practiced in the Prophet's day. The creation of an Islamic state would, according to these people, return Egypt and the broader *ummah*, the vast community of Muslim faithful, to a position of power and prosperity.

It would take another war—a victory—and a bold, visionary leader to restore our pride and position of influence in the region. The change in leadership came before the victory. When Anwar assumed the presidency following Nasser's death in 1970, he wanted to move Egypt toward democracy, which meant the Muslim Brotherhood, as well as other religious and political groups that had proliferated, should be allowed to voice their ideas, their dissent. He released all of the Islamists from prison and eased restrictions, allowing them to publish their newspapers, meet openly, form student unions at the universities, and stage protests. This policy of tolerance would become problematic only after he began making overtures of peace to Israel. After his 1973 victory in the October, or Yom Kippur, War, Anwar could easily have lived on the goodwill this victory generated for the remainder of his career in politics, but that was not my husband's way. Moreover, Anwar knew that even after this triumph—in a war he had sought to avoid but would not shrink from—peace was the greater goal. For a vocal, angry minority, such a peace was unthinkable. Israel was the hated foe against whom we had waged four hard-fought wars in the past thirty years, and for reasons both political and religious, there were those who could not imagine anything other than enmity between our two nations. So

Sadat's announcement in 1977 of his willingness to travel to Jerusalem if necessary, to bring his message directly to the Knesset—the very lair of the enemy—was met with howls of fury in some quarters. As the negotiations continued, eventually culminating in the Camp David Accords and the Egyptian-Israeli treaty for which Sadat and Israeli Premier Menachem Begin were awarded the Nobel Peace Prize in 1979, the furor only intensified. Not only were the Islamists livid, but also few other Arab leaders would openly support Sadat, though there was much behind-the-scenes politicking, something I address at greater length elsewhere in this book.

Despite the protests of the fundamentalists, it was nevertheless obvious that Egypt, Israel, and probably the entire Middle East were desperate for peace. Egypt, in particular, was in the midst of economic crisis, and the money being poured into the defense budget was badly needed for development projects. War was simply too wasteful—in money, in opportunities, in human lives—and no one felt this more acutely than the average Egyptian. As in so many other things, Anwar had the pulse of the people when it came to peace. Upon his return from Jerusalem, he was given a hero's welcome. Millions of Cairenes thronged the streets, literally dancing with joy, to show their support for the president.

Once the treaty with Israel was signed, Anwar was determined to protect the peace that he had fought so hard to achieve, as well as the principles for Palestinian statehood outlined in the Camp David Accords. When, after two years of halting progress, it seemed that there were factions bent on derailing it, he acted, disbanding the various Islamic groups, sweeping many people into prison, and vowing to release them only after the final stage of the Camp David Accords, the return of the Sinai, was complete. For the act, he was harshly criticized by the international community. In truth, what my husband was doing was contrary to his democratic ideals, but a step he believed was necessary to take. Egypt was in a deep crisis: sectarian violence, fanned by radicals of every stripe, was wreaking havoc between Muslims and Christians, and universities were hotbeds of protest orchestrated by angry fundamentalists.

Peace at that time was in a precarious place. Even the Israeli government seemed determined to undermine the agreements that had been hammered out. In 1980, the Knesset passed a basic law declaring Jerusalem the capital of Israel—a violation of international law that was roundly condemned by the United Nations Security Council. In 1981, just two days after a summit meeting with Sadat, Begin authorized the bombing of a nuclear reactor in Baghdad, an action that nearly claimed the peace process as collateral damage. Indeed, two years after the signing of the accords, there was still no commitment to a final peace. Time was running out, and Anwar was afraid that the smallest upset would give Israel an excuse to renege on Begin's promises. I do not say this to justify sweeping detentions: that decision forever marked his presidency and opened him to charges that seemed to undercut his record as a democratic reformer. I do, however, know what it is to be caught in an impossible situation in which national security and personal liberties are at odds.

The detentions did not, however, save Sadat, nor did he intend them to. My husband knew he was a target, and he did not falter in his commitment to peace simply because his life was threatened. It is true that on October 6, 1981, he was murdered by terrorists, but he did not submit to them. The peace for which he gave his life has survived—one triumph in the Middle East's troubled, tragic history.

Similarly, September 11 was a grievous tragedy, but it was not, in fact, a victory for the terrorists. Bin Laden's plot horrified and alienated much of the world, and Americans responded to the crisis with courage and resilience. September 11 did, however, usher in a new and unsettling era, one in which the United States is no longer impregnable, and one, sadly, in which Muslims are too often seen as the enemy: "them" to the civilized world's "us." We are now nearly a decade from that day, and though much lip service has been given to the idea that the War on Terror is not a War on Islam, actions too often speak differently. I know the dangers that fanatics pose, but demonizing the religion of more than 1 billion of the earth's inhabitants is not going to help isolate or root out the zealots. On the contrary, it creates an atmosphere of mutual suspicion and polarization.

Though it seems obvious, it bears repeating that Islam and terrorism do not go hand in hand. I will talk more about the specifics of my faith, which I hold dear, later in this book. Now, however, I think it is important to point out that even the overwhelming majority of Islamists—people who aspire to live in a state guided or administered in accordance with Sharia, Islamic law—do not support political violence. As I mentioned earlier, in the 1990s, Egypt's Muslim Brotherhood agreed to give up all violence. Their pledge has held, and now the Muslim Brotherhood has begun participating in Egypt's civic life. Its ideologies have changed greatly since al-Banna's and Qutb's day, and many of its positions have, by virtue of being exposed to the political process, moderated significantly. And although I do not see eye-to-eye with fanatics, it is not true that Islam and democracy are mutually exclusive. Democracy in Egypt, and indeed, much of the rest of the developing world, is something that needs to arise organically, gradually. The United States has had more than two hundred years to practice refining its political institutions, and they are in line with America's culture and mores. A similar process must take place in Egypt. As we have seen in Iraq, democracy cannot be imposed.

Moreover, we are also seeing that the fight against terrorism is not a simple matter of sorting out who is for democracy or against freedom. The issues are complex and call for subtle understandings of what leads people, of any faith or political leaning (there have been terrorists of all religions and ideologies: Hindu, Jewish, Catholic, Marxist, nationalist, and the list goes on), to resort to such measures. In addition, the struggle against this ancient chimera and modern malaise must be cooperative. Terrorism recognizes no national boundaries, and so it must be fought across borders as a multinational effort. It is not solely America's responsibility to wage the war on terror, nor is it possible for the United States alone to stamp out fanaticism.

In fact, fanaticism cannot be beaten by military means alone. To attack the roots of terrorism in the developing world, we must work to alleviate poverty and illiteracy, the hopelessness, frustration, and lack of opportunity that give militant fundamentalism its terrible allure. In Western Europe and the United States, we must work to reverse the feeling of disenfranchisement that many Muslim immigrants in developed countries experience. Fostering further isolation from the cultural and political mainstream is untenable.

Neither appeasement nor a police state can rid a nation—or the world—of terrorism. I know firsthand that issues of national security and personal liberty are often at odds. I do not believe that civil rights must be eclipsed by the struggle against terror, but long lines at airports, time, and inconvenience are relatively small prices to pay for increased safety. Nor do I rule out eavesdropping on suspected terrorists. Where and how to draw the line is not easy to determine. Political leaders wrestle with this trade-off between security and liberty all the time, just as my husband did thirty years ago. Along the way, however, small efforts to show respect for basic human dignity can make a difference. Two experiences that took place some years ago have come to remind me of the importance of simple courtesy.

I am a legal resident of the United States and am required to renew my green card periodically. I was not surprised that security surrounding this procedure was tighter than it had been before 9/11, but I was taken aback by the way that federal agents treated my fellow legal aliens. Although the officials were unfailingly civil to me—I believe I was afforded special treatment as the wife of a former president—the people around me were addressed rudely, with obvious contempt and suspicion. I was appalled: these were the people who were, by virtue of their very presence there that day, trying to obey the law. If this was the new face of the United States post-9/11, then it was not only the lives lost that day that we should mourn.

On another occasion, I was chagrined to find myself at the heart of a security scare when, just a few weeks after 9/11, I traveled to nearby Lynchburg, Virginia, to receive the Pearl S. Buck Award for promotion of international understanding from Randolph-Macon Woman's College. I noticed that my security detail—sizable given the setting, a bucolic town in southwestern Virginia—was behaving oddly, first carefully managing my movements and then vanishing altogether. Apparently they had been at an emergency FBI briefing: seven Saudi men, alleged to be in Lynchburg on business, had arrived in the city shortly before I did. They were staying at the same hotel where I was lodged, and indeed, on the same floor. An alumna of the college, recently returned from an embassy posting in the Middle East, thought the coincidence ominous. As a result, I was under careful guard. I am accustomed to working with a security detail; in fact, not having one was something I had to get used to after I moved to the United States. When I was the wife of

Anwar Sadat, there were often threats against me. Over time, I grew to be fairly sanguine about these, but the ones against my family never failed to frighten me. Now, however, it seemed unlikely that anyone could hope to gain political leverage by attacking Jehan Sadat, private citizen. Still, the FBI questioned the Saudis, and though satisfied that they were in fact just businessmen in town for a conference, they nevertheless circulated their photos in case they should appear at my lecture.

After all the commotion, I felt both uneasy and awkward. These men had done nothing wrong except come from a country now associated with terrorism. So when, in hushed tones, a few of them were pointed out to me at the hotel, I did the only thing I could: I spoke to them. Four men were in the business center, clustered around computers, reading Arabic newspapers online. The encounter lasted only a few minutes and was not in itself terribly revealing. The older men recognized me instantly; the youngest did not, and all carefully closed out the images of protesting Palestinians they had been looking at. However brief, the simple, respectful exchange that ensued eased the tension, diffused some of the suspicion, and reminded me again of something that Anwar once said—something that I think has great application today, when all too many people are being whipped into a panic about the "Islamic threat" and Muslims have replaced communists as the bogeyman of the West. He said, "Fear is a most effective tool in killing the soul of an individual—and a people."

Islam's Truths and Misconceptions

I BELIEVE THAT EVENTS IN OUR LIVES HAPPEN FOR A PURPOSE, and yet sometimes I marvel at the circumstances that have brought me, in some ways, full circle—face-to-face with a part of my life that I find most painful. When my husband was slain by Islamic extremists, I never imagined that I would one day be living in America, speaking out in an effort to counter the idea that extremists speak for Islam. It would not have occurred to me in 1981 that the example set by my husband's murderers could one day be seen as representative of my faith. Clearly, Islam is facing great challenges— not only from the outside world but from within—and for me, being a good Muslim does not mean abjuring criticism or silencing dissent within our own communities.

Although I am sometimes disheartened, I am not surprised that many Westerners fail to see the true face of Islam. After all, extremists exhort not only their followers to acts of violence, but also the whole *ummah*. Bin Laden, the men who murdered my husband, the blind sheikh, the men who orchestrated the bombings in London and Madrid, Bali and Dahab routinely claim to speak for "the true Islam" or "pure Islam." Not only is this a grievous falsehood, it is a canny manipulation. It is undeniably to their benefit to encourage Westerners to fear and hate all Muslims: these zealots welcome violence, even when waged against them, because it validates their embattled, nihilistic, fight-to-the-death worldview. They would rather people not know how much in opposition to the tenets of Islam their beliefs and actions are. For better or for worse, it has become incumbent on Muslims who repudiate such extremism to speak out—not only to rehabilitate our image in the eyes of the world, but also to safeguard the ideals that Islam enjoins: compassion, social justice, and tolerance. Likewise, it is in the interests of the global community to look beyond the lunatic fringe. To allow some thousands of media-savvy hatemongers to control the discourse surrounding more than a billion people is to empower them mightily.

Earlier in this discussion, I said that peacemaking must not be regarded as solely the work of policymakers. Far too many politicians the world over count on war, or at least the threat of it, to remain relevant; peace would put more than one head of state out of a job. But how can regular citizens—people with busy lives and families to look after, people with more pressing and less overwhelming problems than cooling global tensions—nevertheless cultivate peace? One marvelously simple way is to reject the ubiquitous "clash of civilizations" theory. To view Muslims not as the adversary but in all their multiplicity and realize that as citizens of increasingly pluralistic societies, believing in a paradigm that pits Islam against the West is untenable, not the least because Islam is a large part of the West. There are 5 million Muslims living in the United States and 15 million in Europe. These growing populations must be integrated into the political and civic lives of Western nations, for neither isolation nor total assimilation is a viable option.

The "problem" of Muslim communities in Western Europe—their growing numbers, their sense of alienation from the nations in which they live, and their potential to wreak terror "from the inside"—has become a source of much anxiety. Terms like *Eurabia* and *Londonistan* point to fears that Muslims are trying to take over their "host" nations. Interestingly, such fearmongering does not capture the reality: a 2006 Pew poll on Muslims in the United Kingdom, France, Germany, and Spain finds that Muslims themselves are generally positive about the nations in which they live. In fact, they are more positive than the general publics in all four European countries about the way things are going in their countries. They report both a strong sense of Muslim identity and a willingness to adopt the culture and customs of their host countries, two qualities that should not be seen as mutually exclusive.

Of course, to blame Islam for the problems in immigrant communities is much easier than to attempt to unravel the complex economic and sociological legacies of colonialism. Muslim populations in most Western European nations are there as a result of colonial projects in their homelands, political and economic necessity, or a combination of all three. The riots in France in 2005, 2007, and 2008 led by young men of Arab or North African descent, living in vast ghettos where unemployment is endemic, were less an expression of religion than class. In the same way, the "race riots" that took place in the United States in the late 1960s in places like Los Angeles, Newark, and Detroit were not caused by some aspect of being African American, but rather by social and economic deprivation, a deep-seated sense of injustice, and limited recourse to more legitimate means to air or redress their grievances.

Likewise, the situation of the Turks in Germany, who face great obstacles to obtaining citizenship, and North Africans in Spain is as much about jobs as it is about God. And indeed, the same Pew survey reported, "The greatest concern among Muslim minorities in all four countries is unemployment."

In the United States, where the Muslim population tends to be well-educated professionals, the domestic issues are less acute. In 2006 the Council on American-Islamic Relations (CAIR) conducted a survey of American Muslim voters that revealed the degree to which American Muslims are integrated into American society: they participate politically—89 percent said they vote regularly; they observe national holidays—86 percent said they celebrate the Fourth of July; and they are socially engaged—42 percent said they volunteer for institutions serving the public, as compared to 29 percent nationwide in 2005. Moreover, they do not perceive their religious beliefs to be at odds with those of their fellow citizens: 84 percent said Muslims should strongly emphasize shared values with Christians and Jews, and 77 percent said Muslims worship the same God as Christians and Jews. Nevertheless, despite the overwhelming success of Muslims in the United States, their limited numbers allow them only nominal influence on American perceptions of Islam.

I am not a sociologist or political scientist by training (my doctorate is in comparative literature), so I do not claim that my own measures of public opinion are scientific. However, my work lecturing and speaking in conjunction with the Sadat Chair for Peace and Development at the University of Maryland has allowed me to travel a great deal within the United States, to towns and cities far off the beaten path. Over the past twenty years, I have addressed women's groups, professional organizations, charitable foundations, religious groups, and community centers: I have spoken at leading universities and community colleges, high schools and grammar schools. In short, I have talked to anyone and everyone interested in the idea of peace. I have also listened. As a result, my exposure to the United States has been more comprehensive than one might imagine for a woman whose twin delights are her family and gardening. The opportunity to meet with Americans has been a privilege and a pleasure; this nontraditional student has found her equally nontraditional classroom enriching and instructive. I have learned many things about the United States, and I marvel at the energy, industriousness, and efficiency of the American people. Nevertheless, few people outside major metropolitan areas have significant exposure to Muslims, and thus, on the whole, Islam is unfamiliar and poorly understood.

Recent polls seem to confirm my experience. In a 2007 poll done by Zogby International on American prejudice, 83 percent of 10,000 American adults said that Americans believe Muslims are the most likely of any religious group to engage in terrorism. A 2006 Washington Post/ABC News Poll found that 46 percent of Americans have a negative view of Islam, which was, alarmingly, seven percentage points higher than their poll conducted in 2001—just after the September 11 attacks. A 2006 Gallup poll on American beliefs about Muslims living in the United States reported that 39 percent of respondents believed that Muslims are not loyal to the United States.

Meanwhile, the Pew Forum on Religion and Public Life 2007 poll reported that 58 percent of respondents say they know little or nothing about Islam's practices. When asked for the single word that best describes their impression of Islam, far more Americans mention negative words than positive ones (30 percent versus 15 percent); almost a quarter (23 percent) characterize the religion with neutral words; about a third (32 percent) do not offer an opinion. Fully 70 percent of non–Muslims say that the Muslim religion is very different from their own religion, compared with just 19 percent who say Islam and their own religion have a lot in common. Two years ago, 59 percent viewed Islam as very different from their own religion. And in November 2001, just 52 percent expressed this view.

There is no shortage of excellent information about Islam, but for people to avail themselves of it, they may need to look beyond the superficial coverage on TV, where the same shot of angry men in turbans seems to accompany every story, and talk radio, in which most mentions of Muslims are made by political rabble-rousers inveighing against what they say are our insidious plans to take over the world. Obviously there are exceptions, but for the most part, what the news showcases is not the whole story. This is doubly true for those who, without constraint, air their opinions on the Internet, where anti-Muslim bigotry is but a click away. This is problematic, because as the Pew Forum reports: "The biggest influence on the public's impressions of Muslims, particularly among those who express an unfavorable opinion of Muslims, is what people hear and read in the media. About a third of the public (32 percent)—including nearly half of those who offer a negative opinion of Muslims (48 percent)—say what they have seen or read in the media has had the biggest influence on their views. Other factors, such as personal experience and education, are less influential, though they are cited far more often by those who have favorable impressions of Muslims than those who express negative views."

Pew further reported that more than half of the American public now believes the "terrorist attacks over the last few years are, or soon will be, part of a major civilizational conflict between Islam and the West." I find it unfortunate that while many of the policies that took root in post-9/11 America, including the doctrine of preemption and the forcible spread of democracy, have been relegated to the junk heap of history, the "clash of civilizations" theory, which provides the ideological underpinnings for all of the above, has not been discredited. In the interests of hastening its demise, I present misconceptions that, in my experience, represent the major points of misunderstanding about Islam.

First, however, I will establish a few basics. Most people (with the exception of 10 percent of Americans who, according to the CAIR survey, believe that Muslims worship a "moon god") know that Muslims believe in "Allah," which is simply the Arabic name for "One and Only God." Indeed, Arab Christians use the same word. He is the same God who made a covenant with Abraham, appeared to Moses in the burning bush, tested Job, and dispatched Jesus to preach his truth. In Europe and America, people talk about the Judeo-Christian tradition, yet Islam is also part of this tradition and indeed shares many of the fundamental tenets set down in the Torah and the Gospels. In deference to this common heritage, Jews and Christians, known as "People of the Book," are accorded special respect in Islam: "We believe in God and that which is revealed to us; and that which was revealed unto Abraham and Ishmael and Isaac and Jacob and the tribes, and that which Moses and Jesus received, and that which the prophets received from their Lord. We make no distinction between any of them, and to God, we have surrendered ourselves" (Qur'an, 2:136).

Many Christians are still somewhat surprised to learn that Muslims believe in Jesus, who, along with other Christian saints such as John the Baptist and the Virgin Mary, are important and beloved figures in Islam. We revere Jesus as one of a succession of messengers, beginning with Adam and ending with Mohammed, the "Seal of the Prophets," who have, throughout history, transmitted the fundamental truth of God to humans. We do not, however, recognize Jesus as the Son of God, for in contrast to the Christian idea of the Trinity, we believe in the oneness of God: "Say, God is One; the Eternal God; He begot none, nor was He begotten; none is equal to Him" (Qur'an, 112:1–4).

Moreover, we believe that God's final, perfect revelation was given, via the angel Gabriel, to a man named Mohammed ibn Abdullah, an Arab of the Quraysh tribe living in what is now Saudi Arabia. This revelation, which was made—verse by magnificent verse—over a period of twenty-two years beginning in 610 C.E., is the Qur'an, which for Muslims is the direct word of God. Filled with divine messages of inspiration and instruction that cover all aspects of life, the Qur'an is both a continuation and a correction of the earlier revelations, which Muslims believe had been corrupted over time by human interpretation. Because the truth imparted by Mohammed was not new, he cannot be said to be the "founder" of Islam, as some have called him. Nor, it is important to point out, do Muslims worship our Prophet, as the old-fashioned label "Mohammedans" implied. We worship only God. We do, however, aspire to emulate Mohammed in all ways, for he is the exemplar of the perfect Islam, or submission to God's will. How a Muslim should live is defined by how Mohammed did live, and so Muslims rely on the Hadith and Sunna, the collected sayings of the Prophet, his practice and traditions.

Muslims believe in an afterlife and the Day of Judgment, when each person, without exception, must stand alone and answer to God for the way he has chosen to live out his time on earth. "Believers, be they Jewish, Sabean, and Christian—whoever believes in God and the Last Day and does what is right—shall have nothing to fear or to regret" (Qur'an, 5:69). Muslims are often misrepresented as fatalists, hidebound by notions of predestination, but this is fallacious. We believe no human being is without conscience and intent; therefore, we are responsible for our own actions. Indeed, Islam shows the way, but it is the individual who must do the hard work and follow the straight path. In contrast to the Christian idea that—because of Eve's transgression—humankind has fallen, Islam believes that people are fundamentally good; the Qur'an (2:30) calls humans God's "vice-regents" on earth.

At its heart, Islam requires participation and belief in five specific practices, known as the pillars of Islam:

1. The Declaration of Faith, *Shahada,* which is a two-line statement: "There is no God but God and Mohammed is his Prophet." So essential is this to Islam that in order to become a Muslim, one must repeat this five times in front of two witnesses.
2. Prayer, *Salat,* is the performance of five obligatory prayers each day facing toward Mecca. These prayers are the foundation of a Muslim's personal relationship with God.
3. Almsgiving, *Zakat,* is a mandatory annual charity to the poor. It is a testament to the central role of social justice in Islam.
4. Fasting, *Saum,* occurs during the month of Ramadan when from first light until sunset, Muslims refrain from food, drink, acts of physical intimacy, tobacco, cursing, and quarreling. We fast in order to purify ourselves, learn self-discipline, and identify with the poor and hungry.
5. Pilgrimage, *Hajj,* is an obligation to pray and perform religious rituals in the holy city of Mecca, the birthplace of Islam, for those physically and financially able.

It is worth noting that all of the above are practices, not merely ideas or concepts. The religious scholar Karen Armstrong talks about Islam as an "orthopraxy" as well as an "orthodoxy," and the centrality of behavior in Islam. This is not to say that mechanical repetition of actions sanctioned by God should be mistaken for piety. On the contrary, the intention, or *niyya,* of a believer is essential in Islam: without the correct intention, a religious devotion is meaningless; with intention, even the most ordinary activity is transformed into an act of worship. This marks an important difference between Islam and many other religious traditions, and it has important implications. Islam draws no distinction between sacred and profane, private and public, spiritual and material. Instead, it provides a blueprint for living that encompasses the entirety of one's existence and governs and guides every aspect of a Muslim's life according to clear moral, spiritual, and physical rules and standards. At its most practical and straightforward core, the basic moral principle in Islam is that that which is good is permitted and that which is harmful is not permitted.

It is, above all, a faith for human beings with all our faults and blemishes. We are not called on to renounce the world but to live ordinary lives as a part of it, practicing moderation in all things. Extremism runs counter to the core principles of Islam; nevertheless, in the minds of too many people, these two words—*extremism* and *Islam*—are linked. And that brings me to the misconceptions about Islam.

Misconception 1:
Islam Is Monolithic

Whether by accident or design, the discussions surrounding Islam imply that it is somehow homogeneous, that Muslims behave in lockstep, identical in belief, ideology, and agenda. The mind-set pitting Islam against the West facilitates such an illusion; the truth, of course, is quite different. Muslims make up 1.2 billion of the earth's inhabitants, and they live in many more places than the Middle East. In fact, though "Muslim" and "Arab" are often used interchangeably, less than 20 percent of the world's Muslims are Arabs. And even among this subsection, which is ostensibly linked by a common language, there exist profound cultural, ethnic, and political differences. The culture that developed in Egypt's agrarian Nile basin is far removed from the tribal desert nomadism that took hold in Jordan. And these differences are not limited to our ancient pasts. Speaking as someone who had a front row seat to the pan-Arab movement, achieving any practical unity of goals among our member nations was challenging indeed. Thus, to think that Muslims in China, Indonesia, South and Central Asia, and Eastern Europe, as well as Western Europe and North America, are homogeneous is to misunderstand human beings. Cultural and regional differences abound: it stands to reason that Muslims in Bosnia might have a different worldview than, say, Muslims in Somalia, just as Mexican Catholics and Irish Catholics are not identical although both look to Rome for spiritual guidance.

This brings me to my next point: there is no Islamic pope who can speak on behalf of all the faithful, and in the majority Sunni tradition no ecclesiastical hierarchy that might constitute an Islamic version of "the Church." Occasionally I hear Al-Azhar, the ancient university in Cairo and the leading center of Sunni tradition, likened to the Vatican, but this is inaccurate. Islamic sheikhs and imams are not analogous to Christian preachers or priests or Jewish rabbis. In Sunni Islam, a sheikh is a religious scholar, and an imam is one who has been chosen to lead the believers in prayer— a selection resulting from the imam's knowledge of the Qur'an, his age, and his stature within the community. Sheikhs and imams do not act as intercessors, and Muslims are under no obligation to obey them. The individual's relationship with God is a direct one. Some Muslims may be better qualified to interpret Muslim doctrine or practice—the traditions of scholarship surrounding the Qur'an are multiple, complex, and ancient—nevertheless, all Muslims are fundamentally equal.

Somewhat ironically, it is this sort of decentralization of authority that may account for part of the reason that Americans and Europeans believe that Muslim leaders have failed to speak out against terrorism. In fact, Muslims *have*—but such statements arrive from many quarters. After 9/11, after the bombings in London, Madrid, and elsewhere where innocent blood has been spilled, Muslims have issued condemnations. Whether such denunciations receive as much attention as more incendiary anti-Western messages is another question entirely. Once again, when we frame the encounter between Muslims and non-Muslims as a clash between extremist Orientals and enlightened Occidentals, we have a tendency to select the stories that will fit inside that framework and sideline the rest.

The monolith myth is further undermined by the fact that there are different traditions within Islam, the best known and widely misunderstood being the division between Sunni and Shiite. In 2006, a man named Jeff Stein, the national security editor at the United States *Congressional Quarterly*, flummoxed members of United States House intelligence committees by asking whether they could identify the difference between a Sunni and a Shiite. They could not. Nor did they know to which camp Hezbollah *and* almost all Iranians belong. (In fact, both Iranians and Hezbollah are Shiite.) Perhaps most disturbing was the fact that this whole discussion was couched in terms of "knowing the enemy." It is primarily as a consequence of the Iraq war that most Americans have encountered the Sunni and Shia traditions, but the appalling sectarian violence that has taken place in the wake of the overthrow of Saddam Hussein and subsequent de-Baathification of Iraq is in no way representative of the general state of affairs between the sects.

The split between Sunni and Shiite has its roots in a dispute concerning the rightful successor to the Prophet Mohammed. When the Prophet died in 632, he left no male heir; thus, most Muslims looked to his father-in-law to assume leadership of the nascent Muslim community. A passionate few believed the caliphate belonged to Ali, the Prophet's son-in-law, and thereafter his direct descendants. Those who support the succession as it took place, from Mohammed to the first four "Rightly Guided" caliphs and beyond, are called Sunni Muslims, from the word *Sunnah*, the tradition of the Prophet. Today, we Sunnis comprise 85 percent of the world's Muslims. This, the tradition in which I was raised, is closest to what the Prophet himself practiced and is considered the orthodox version of Islam. Orthodoxy does not, however, imply rigidity or homogeneity. On the contrary, even the most ancient and scholarly traditions of Islamic thought allow room for disagreement. Egypt in particular is renowned for its pluralistic, tolerant interpretation of Islam. This is undoubtedly a function of our history. Unlike the vast and forbidding Arabian Desert, which was for the most part unconquerable, Egypt has been attracting people—and rulers—from the world over for thousands of years. Our traditions of cosmopolitanism and tolerance date back thousands of years: religious pluralism is part of the Egyptian identity. Today, Copts, an Orthodox Christian sect that traces its Christianity to St. Mark, comprise 10 percent of Egypt's population. For much of our history, Muslim, Christian, and Jewish communities in Egypt have coexisted peacefully, but this changed when the war over Suez in 1956 caused many Jews to leave the country.

Because of their conviction that leadership of the *ummah* must remain in the Prophet's own line, Shia Muslims—Shi'at Ali, or Party of Ali—have not recognized the authority of elected Muslim leaders, following instead a line of imams, of which Ali was the first. The Shia imamate, in contrast to the Sunni caliphate, is a religious office as well as a political one. Whereas caliphs regarded their power as temporal, the imams were "divinely inspired, sinless, infallible, religio-political" leaders, according to Akbar Ahmed, author of *Islam Today*. There are other differences in Sunni and Shiite approaches to Islamic jurisprudence and their interpretations of history that are beyond the scope of this book to explore, but both Sunni and Shiite practice the five pillars of Islam and regard one another as Muslims.

Today, the Shia are concentrated in Iran, southern Iraq, and southern Lebanon, with significant Shiite communities in Saudi Arabia and Syria, Kuwait, Yemen, Bahrain, Afghanistan, Pakistan, and India as well. It is through these three nations—Iran, Iraq, and Lebanon—that some Mideast leaders and policy advisers worry that a Shiite crescent will form—a chain of Shiite governments and political movements with the authority to alter the traditional balance of power between the two main Islamic sects that might possibly destabilize the region. It is true that the relations between the leadership of some Sunni-majority nations and Shiite governments and parties is strained, but this is not true across the board, and it does not reflect doctrinal differences so much as political ones. Ironically, the political system in Iran, where the leadership presumes to speak for God, is often pointed to by the fundamentalists as the model for an ideal Islamic state. Nothing could be further from the truth.

Iran bears additional mention since it was there, in 1979, that the phobia of Islam in its most recent iteration took seed. Prior to this, for most Americans, Islam was little more than a remote, mysterious, and largely ignored religion, something superficially studied in a world history course. This changed when the faces of the Iranian captors and their American captives stared at the world from our television screens and front pages of newspapers and magazines. Again and again, the hostage takers were described not as Iranian students but as Muslims, whereas the hostages were simply American citizens, with no religious affiliations appended. There was no attempt to distinguish between a religion and the perpetrators of a lawless, politically motivated act. This would, tragically, establish a precedent for journalistic coverage that has not yet been broken.

There is also a third tradition in Islam that bears noting—one that gets considerably more positive, though not necessarily more accurate, press: that of the Sufis. The Sufis are not a sect, but instead the mystics of Islam who seek intimate knowledge of God through contemplation, ritual, and spiritual exercises. Perhaps the Sufi best known in the West is the poet Jalal al-Din Rumi, whose Mevlevi order in Turkey is sometimes called the whirling dervishes and whose verses are beloved by spiritual seekers of many religions.

Tolerant—for they seek truth in all faiths and see God in everyone and everything—esoteric, and sometimes ascetic, Sufi orders coalesce around a learned master, or sheikh, who can instruct them in the mysteries and disciplines of this innermost journey. As in many other spiritual traditions, suppression of the ego is regarded as a necessary first step to the experience of transcendence. At various points in history, Sufism has run afoul of orthodox Muslim authorities. Islam has no monastic tradition, because Muslims believe that it is within the community, not in withdrawal from it, that God is served. So some fundamentalist strains in Islam find the Sufi practices heterodox. Nevertheless, their influence has been considerable. Many of the great Muslim jurists and leaders were Sufis, and some traditions describe the companions of the Prophet as Sufis. Sufi traders in South Asia, West Africa, Indonesia, and Malaya (Malaysia) are generally credited with introducing Islam to the local populations. It is worth noting that the spread of Islam in Indonesia, the largest Muslim democracy in the world, had nothing whatsoever to do with military conquest. Even today, the ideas of Sufism continue to attract converts to Islam.

Obviously it is beyond the scope of this book to catalogue all of the facets of Islam. Furthermore, it is not my intention to disprove the myth of the monolith by portraying Muslims as fractious or divided—for it is the sense of brotherhood despite our vast differences that is part of the genius of Islam—but to share something of the history, richness, and variety of my religion.

Several years ago, I noted with interest the drafting of something called the Amman message, which seems to me to reflect both the multiplicity and unity of Islam. In 2004, King Abdullah II of Jordan sent three questions to twenty-four of the most senior Muslim scholars in the world, representing all the branches and schools of Islam: (1) Who is a Muslim? (2) Is it permissible to declare someone an apostate (*takfir*)? (3) Who has the right to undertake issuing *fatwas* (legal rulings)?

Based on the *fatwas* provided by these scholars—including the sheikh of Al-Azhar, Sunni Islam's highest authority, a number of the foremost Shi'i ayatollahs, as well as the most senior religious authorities of Muslim nations—in July 2005, an international Islamic conference of two hundred of the world's leading Islamic scholars was convened in Amman. There, these scholars, who hail from different nations and traditions, unanimously issued rulings on three seminal issues. First, they affirmed the fundamental validity of all of the eight traditional and authoritative schools of Islamic jurisprudence; second, they categorically denounced the practice of *takfir*, or declaring a fellow Muslim an apostate; and third, they clarified who has the right to issue *fatwas* in the name of Islam. Since then, the message has been signed by some five hundred scholars, sheikhs, and heads of state, among them Sunnis, Shiites, Sufis, and, indeed, representatives of every Muslim tradition. It is only one example of scores of significant (and, in the West, underreported) ways in which the *ummah* is acting to repudiate the wanton violence committed in its name.

Misconception 2:
Islam Incites Terrorism and Is a Violent Faith

This is patently false; nevertheless, at least a fifth of American people believe this is true, according to the CAIR survey. Terrorism is ecumenical and nonpartisan and has been used by groups of different political and religious persuasions. Historically, terror is a hallmark of asymmetric conflict, wielded by a weaker party against a dominant power over whom they cannot hope to prevail. Thus, they strike out in ways that will frighten, demoralize, and, ideally, weaken their enemy. The fact that some terrorists have been Muslims reveals less about the tenets of Islam than about the social and political position of those who resort to these tactics, just as Irish Republican Army bombings provide little commentary on the teachings of Catholicism, and the assassination of Israeli prime minister Yitzak Rabin by an ultraorthodox zealot is not a window on Judaism. Indeed, in the young man who shot Rabin, with his posturing before the cameras, his quoting of Torah to justify his actions, and his determination to derail the fragile peace process between Israel and Palestine, I saw the image of the Muslim fanatics who killed my husband. The resonances were both frightening and painful, for I had come to know Rabin and his wife, Leah, quite well, and they stand as a vivid illustration that zealots of all faiths are essentially alike, for they betray the very God they claim to serve.

The Muslim idea of *jihad* has become distorted beyond recognition, so much so that I fear its original meaning will be forever lost. Through selective readings and reinterpretation of Islam's holy injunctions, fanatics have twisted it to mean violence directed at whomever they choose. Even prior to 9/11, which made *jihad* a household term, Western writers and filmmakers were misusing it in their efforts to create a sensational, stereotyped villain: a backward, bloodthirsty barbarian who "prays and kills," a new bad guy to replace the Soviet archenemy—or perhaps, as some argue, revive a far older one. (That the Crusades have so often been invoked in the discussion of the relationship between Islam and the West is disheartening, to say the least.) Terrorists use the word in part because they know it is familiar and frightening to Westerners. So given the fact that its meaning has largely been altered, why is it important to draw a distinction? Because the practice and belief in jihad are, in fact, a part of Islam, and so long as there are non-Muslims convinced that jihad is synonymous with the taking of innocent lives, they will remain convinced that such actions, which are anathema to Muslims, are condoned by Islam.

Many experts have pointed out that jihad means struggle, and not necessarily the sort that is conducted with weapons. In fact, there is a famous Hadith of the Prophet that talks about returning from a military war, which he called the "lesser jihad," to the "greater jihad," namely, the effort to built a just and equitable society. Still, Western nervousness about jihad does not revolve around Islamic community building, but rather "holy war," which is how, until recently, jihad has been translated and understood. But as scholars Imam Feisal Abdul Rauf and Reza Aslan point out, a more accurate analogue to jihad is the Western concept of a "just war." Indeed, the Qur'an and Hadith are clear in supporting armed struggle only as a last resort in order to defend against military aggression.

Moreover, complex preconditions must be met for the declaration of an armed jihad: Islam must be in dire danger and jihad must end when the threat to Islam no longer exists. Only the entire community of religious authorities can declare jihad; ordinary men cannot declare it in the name of Islam. *Never* can Muslims wage jihad against other Muslims. Nonbelievers must be permitted to either accept Islam or request protection within Islam. Jihad is a serious, extensively and intensely contemplated procedure. *There has been no call for jihad against the West and Christianity.* Terrorist groups like al Qaeda, and before them, the blind sheikh's Islamic Group, who have urged Muslims to make holy war against the West, have no authority to do so. Furthermore, they will kill Muslims as easily as they will kill anyone else who refuses to believe as they do.

Jihad is not a political action that can be declared by a political leader as a means to satisfy his own objectives: bin Laden has no authority to declare jihad, nor does Zawahiri. Wanton, indiscriminate violence is neither a religious requirement nor even a characteristic of Islam. Peace, above all else, is the goal of Islam. Belief in Islam is not forced on its followers by either the sword or submachine gun. Never! All believers know that our Holy Book says, "There shall be no compulsion in religion. True guidance is now distinct from error. He that renounces idol-worship and puts his faith in God shall grasp a firm handle that will never break. God hears all and knows all" (Qur'an, 2:256).

Suicide bombers are anathema to Islam, which not only instructs us to love life, but clearly states that our souls are not ours to destroy—much less the innocent souls of others. The Qur'an plainly states that killing an innocent person is tantamount to killing all mankind. Those who urge young men and women to use themselves as weapons are *not* preaching Islam. Nor are suicide bombers necessarily Muslims: secular Palestinian groups have resorted to similar tactics, and it was a Sri Lankan separatist group, the Tamil Tigers, that perfected the use of the suicide bomb as an assassination tool in the 1980s and 1990s. The common denominator is not a shared faith, but rather an overwhelming sense of grievance, powerlessness, and hatred. Robert Pape, an expert on suicide bombing and the author of *Dying to Win,* has studied the phenomenon for many years. In analyzing Tamil, Palestinian, Chechen, and al Qaeda suicide bombers, Pape found that what they had most in common was a perception that their communities were being humiliated by more powerful outsiders and that they could reverse that humiliation by inflicting pain on those countries and forcing them to withdraw. In an editorial in the *Chicago Tribune,* he wrote, "Suicide terrorism is a tactic, not an enemy, and beneath the religious rhetoric with which it is perpetrated, it occurs largely in the service of secular aims. Suicide terrorism is mainly a response to foreign occupation rather than a product of Islamic fundamentalism."

The 2008 Arab Opinion Poll, conducted under the auspices of the Sadat Chair and Zogby International, shows little support for al Qaeda's methods or global goals. When asked what aspects of al Qaeda they sympathized with most, if any, only 7 percent of Arabs polled identified its advocacy of a puritanical Islamic state, while 10 percent identified its methods. This seems a clear indication of something most Arabs know: a state shaped according to al Qaeda's vision of Islam is profoundly unappealing, and the means by which they promote their agenda—indiscriminate murder—are unacceptable. However, a plurality identified al Qaeda's willingness to stand up to the United States as the aspect of the organization that they were sympathetic to. This too merits discussion. For even as it appears that sympathy for extremism is steadily decreasing, antipathy toward the United States is strong—indeed overwhelming. But as the Sadat Chair Poll found, 80 percent said that their feeling toward the United States was based on American policy, versus only 12 percent who cited American values. A wide-ranging Gallup Poll on the Muslim world echoes this data. "The conflict with the United States is about policy, not principles," according to Dalia Mogahed, the executive director of the Gallup Center for Muslim Studies.

These public opinion measures confirm what I know to be true. Arabs do not agree with the blind allegiance of the United States to Israel when the situation demands impartiality. The occupation of the Palestinian people and their suffering has not been alleviated despite the visits and promises of Western leaders.

Misconception 3:
Islam Is Against Democracy

Because Islamic countries, unlike Europe, have become more religious and less secular in recent decades, Islam is sometimes accused of being backward. Nowhere is this more evident than in the discussions of Muslims and democracy. Granted, there are some fundamentalists who argue that a system in which the people are sovereign undermines the preeminence of God, but this is an issue with all forms of government, not just democracies. There are also a few who reject it categorically because it seems a Western invention, and therefore suspect. Most experts, however, agree that Muslims by and large are interested in and open to representational government. The Gallup Muslim World poll reports that in the ten predominantly Muslim nations polled—Egypt, Pakistan, Saudi Arabia, Jordan, Bangladesh, Morocco, Indonesia, Iran, Turkey, and Lebanon—what Muslims most admire about the West, after technology, is its political freedom. It further indicates that if their country were drafting a constitution today, overwhelming majorities in these same countries would support freedom of speech, religion, and assembly. Majorities in virtually every country also felt women should have the same legal rights as men.

To me, this makes perfect sense. Muslims are enjoined to live a life of brotherhood without distinction. We are to respect and treat all human beings as equals regardless of creed or color, whether men or women, civilians or soldiers, rulers or subjects, rich or poor. Islam is, in fact, a spiritual democracy, radically egalitarian, and deeply concerned with human dignity.

Moreover, as scholar John Esposito writes in *Political Islam*, "Traditional Islamic concepts and institutions that can be seen as compatible with democracy: these include consultation *(shura)* of rulers with those ruled, consensus *(ijma')* of the community, a long tradition of free scholarly debate and interpretation *(ijtihad)*, and legal principles such as the public welfare *(maslaha)* of society to develop Islamic forms of parliamentary governance, representative elections, and religious reform." The idea of the consent of the governed is also present in Sunni Islam: in "Islam and the Challenge of Democracy," Khaled Abou El Fadl points out that the caliphate must be based on a contract between the caliph and the people who give their *bay'a*, or consent, in return for his promise to discharge the terms of the contract.

So why does such a perception persist? The issue arises on the thorny question of the absolute separation of religion and governance. Because Islam regards the whole of life as holy, it is difficult for Muslims to embrace political philosophies that attempt to create what we see as an artificial division between religious and secular activities. Islam guides us toward right conduct not only on an individual level, but also in terms of the community, and so to jettison God's instructions for the creation of a just society is, by definition, something few Muslims are willing to do. This does not mean that all Muslims aspire to live in a theocratic state, or one in which Sharia is the sole law of the land. It does, however, mean that a democracy in a Muslim majority country will be built on Islamic values and look different from its wholly secular, Western counterpart. Indeed, this is as it should be: history demonstrates that simply importing and applying a political system wholesale is a recipe for failure.

The Western secular tradition took centuries to emerge, and it reflects the particular culture and values of its people. The same thing can happen in other parts of the world. Many scholars, including Khaled Abou El Fadl, Imam Feisal Abdul Rauf, and Ali S. Asani, have pointed out that absolute secularism is not the foundation of democracy; religious pluralism is. And Islam has a mighty tradition of such pluralism. Support for this comes directly from the Qur'an, which states that God deliberately created diverse traditions so that humans might learn from one another: "And for each of you, We have made a law and a practice; and if God wanted He would have made you a single people. But that He may try you by that which He hath given you. So vie with each other in good works. Unto God ye will all return, and He will then inform you of that wherein ye differed" (Qur'an, 5:48).

This pluralism has also been borne out by history. In Muslim lands, Jews and Christians were allowed to live peacefully and productively. Forced conversions are anathema to Islam; Mohammed's injunction that there is no compulsion in religion is one of the central tenets of our faith. Moreover, Mohammed believed that Jews and Christians have valid revelations of their own. Perhaps the greatest examples of Islam's pluralist tradition were the Muslim kingdoms of medieval Spain, which were marked by religious tol-

erance for Christians and Jews, enlightened rule, and an environment of intellectual and material progress. Scholars, both European
and Arab, have pointed to the kingdom of Córdoba as the shining
example of a just and tolerant Islamic state. In an article on religious pluralism in Islam, Ali Asani, a professor at Harvard and a
Kenyan Muslim of South Asian ancestry, writes,

> From the earliest periods of Muslim history we have examples
> of a great deal of respect for the rights of non-Muslims under
> Muslim rule. For instance, the fourth Caliph Ali ibn Abi Talib
> (d. 661) instructed his governor in Egypt to show mercy, love
> and kindness for all subjects under his rule, including non-
> Muslims whom he declared to be 'your equals in creation.'
> Such tolerance is later reflected in the policies of the Arab
> dynasties of Spain, the Fatimids in North Africa, and the Turk-
> ish Ottomans in the Middle East granting maximum individ-
> ual and group autonomy to those adhering to a religious
> tradition other than Islam.

Interestingly, Asani, an American citizen who describes himself as
"a pluralist Muslim," writes, "I am struck by the resonance between
the pluralism espoused in the Qur'an and that in the constitution
and civic culture of the United States."

My ideas about democracy in a Muslim majority nation are not
simply theoretical; they were formed through difficult, hard-won
experience. My husband dreamed of democracy for our country,
and when he succeeded to the presidency after Gamal Abdel
Nasser's death, he set out to make that dream come true. As a
devout Muslim, he knew there is no contradiction between Islam
and democracy. Sadat loved Nasser as his brother and fellow patriot,
but with time, he determined that Nasser's socialistic policies were

not in the best interests of the Egyptian people. Sadat's intent was to take Egypt on a very different journey: "I think that politics is the art of building up a society wherein the will of God is enacted. In such a society as that, each individual should enjoy absolute freedom, subject to no other restrictions than those implicit in the genuine human values of society itself. An individual should never feel that he is at the mercy of any force or coercion or that his will is subordinated to those of others."

As I mentioned earlier, Sadat allowed protests on the university campus, fostered a free press, and established a multiparty system. For a time, Egypt seemed to be moving closer and closer to democracy, even though fundamentalists were now within their rights to deliver messages contrary to Egypt's tradition of tolerance to hundreds of thousands attending our universities. They were insisting that Sharia be our only code of law; that Egypt no longer accept imports from the West; that the Qur'an forbade peace with Israel; that Copts were enemies of Muslims; and that men and women could not attend university together.

Granted, their positions were abhorrent to the vast majority of Egyptians; however, their hate-filled rhetoric did fuel sectarian violence between Muslim and Copt. It was a frightening time, not least because the peace process hung in the balance. Although he could have silenced his critics and reinstated the old restrictions, Anwar did not. Instead he instituted economic reforms aimed specifically at the middle class and young people despite the fact that Egypt was in economic crisis. Egypt needed to modernize its economy, and whenever a nation embarks on a new path, there are painful repercussions. For us, there were riots when subsidies to essential commodities were lifted. In addition, Sadat was making peace with Israel, another bold change for the country. The summer of 1981 was a crucial time for Egypt as our financial, social, and political institutions were being sorely tested. Sadat was determined to weather the storm—to give us a more stable economy and peace.

Meanwhile in Iran, the Ayatollah Khomeini had come to power, and militant Islamists in Egypt admired these events. They were, however, our friends, and to leave them twisting in the wind, as so many other erstwhile allies had done, would have been totally opposed to the basic tenets of Islam. Even if we had not known them personally, our decision would have been the same. Worst of all was the steadily building tension between Muslim and Copt, which in the spring and summer of 1981 exploded into violence. Our nations seemed poised at the edge of fiery conflagration, with fanatics on both sides fanning the flames.

Such were the events leading up to Sadat's detention of Egypt's dissidents. I say this not as a means of excusing it, but rather to place it in context. On September 5, 1981, Anwar ordered the arrest of fifteen hundred people—anyone who might have had a role in the recent religious violence. These included fundamentalist sheikhs, Coptic priests, members of the Muslim Brotherhood, communists, and many others. Once he had ordered the arrests, he insisted that they be conducted openly—so openly that the names of the detainees were published in the newspapers so their loved ones would know where they were. Furthermore, the detainees' relatives were allowed to visit them in jail. In Anwar's mind, such extreme action served as a protective and precautionary move. He saw no other way to keep the peace train on track. Time was running out, and the smallest upset would have spoiled everything. Israel would have been handed an excuse for Begin to renege on Israel's promises. Anwar never intended to use this imprisonment to silence any opposition directed at him and his peace initiative; nevertheless, he could not permit a small group of dissidents to alter the course of peace for our country. I know that to Americans and Europeans, this kind of reasoning seems inexcusable; the West sees an action against democracy, as it understands democracy, as especially repressive to Americans and their First Amendment.

Anwar was harshly criticized, and I know he acutely felt the condemnation. He admired the United States and wanted democracy for our country. Had Sadat lived—had he been able to follow through on his plans to free the political dissidents the moment after the return of Sinai was complete and to step down from the presidency after two terms in office—perhaps things might have been different. There is, one realizes, always a world of "perhapses"— but little utility in such speculation. I do know, however, that a fully functioning democracy is well worth pursuing.

My hope for Egypt is that despite the significant challenges, we will continue to strive to create a culture and polity that fosters participation, reflects and preserves Egyptian values of tolerance and respect for family, and allows us to compete in an innovative, technologically advanced global marketplace. In my mind, education is the key to this: more than one-third of our population is under the age of fifteen, and Egypt's educational resources cannot possibly keep abreast of the demand. The government is building new schools, renovating old ones, training teachers, providing them with equipment like computers, while simultaneously trying to stamp out adult illiteracy, but these initiatives take huge influxes of money, and Egypt, though rich in culture, is a poor nation. The idea that terrorism is a result of poverty and illiteracy has been disputed of late, and analysts have pointed to the upper-middle-class backgrounds of terrorist leaders like bin Laden and Zawahiri as evidence. But this is true of most extremist movements, which are articulated and led by intellectuals and educated people who wish to tear down the status quo and remake it according to their own, often bloody, vision. And these men would have little influence if they did not have a cadre of young men (and some women) who are disaffected, uneducated, or educated and underemployed, lacking in opportunity, parochial in their outlook, with whom their message of alienation resonates. Illiteracy, poverty, prejudice: these, not Islam, are the enemy. Imagine a global war on poverty. This alone would do more to cripple the cause of terror than any military intervention.

My Own Faith

O F ALL THE INSTANCES OF CULTURE SHOCK THAT MOVING
to the United States occasioned—and there were many—strangest
of all was that I was living in a place that did—and does—not know
the expression *insha'allah*. True, I have heard American and British
friends punctuate their statements with an occasional "God willing,"
which is what *insha'allah* means, but I daresay it is not quite the same
thing. In Egypt, it is an expression that is relied on so utterly, repeated
so continually and universally—invoked on the quiet, dusty paths
of rural villages and on the crowded streets of Cairo alike—that it
is a part of our national character. For Egyptian Muslims (and many
Christians, too), *insha'allah* is the constant reminder that human
beings are not in control. It is funny, but also somewhat telling, that
most foreigners and visitors to Egypt believe it means "never."

One evening when a friend of mine from the States and I were
on our way to the Cairo Opera House, she became quite upset
when we came to a standstill in traffic. Worried, she asked the driver,

"Are you sure we will we be there when the curtain rises?" The driver responded, "*Insha'allah!*" Knowing what she was thinking when I saw the disappointed look on her face, I began laughing as I explained what he really meant. "Oh, yes, I see. God willing," she replied without much conviction.

Our habit of saying *insha'allah* is, to my mind, a reflection of the deeply religious feeling that permeates every aspect of a Muslim's life, a conscious acceptance of human fallibility and steadfast belief in the omnipotent, omnipresent will of God. Even if we know that something cannot be done, we will say *insha'allah* to voice our belief or hope beyond hope that, God willing, a miracle may happen. Some people have dismissed our use of *insha'allah* as mere superstition or wishful thinking, but I disagree. To me, *insha'allah* symbolizes the highest expression of faith: a Muslim's sustaining acceptance of the will of God, no matter what the outcome.

This is not to say that such acceptance is always easy. After Anwar was killed, I struggled mightily. His death shook me to my very foundations, and for a long time, I could do little. I did not want to leave our home, to work on my beloved projects, to be involved in life outside my own grief. Yet, in the depths of my being, I knew that I had to go on: God had given me life, and I, in turn, had to do something of value with it. I had to believe in His will, and I did. I always will. Eventually, through prayer, meditation, and the unstinting love and support of my family and friends, I was able to emerge from this excruciating grief. Indeed, I was able to emerge with a new and growing sense of the purpose of my life: to practice Islam, to work for peace.

Faith has always played an essential role in my life. My mother, a British Christian woman who had married a Muslim, made sure that her children understood their father's religion and how to practice its rituals. Of course, our mother could not teach us these rituals, so she turned our religious education over to our father's family. Yet, being a British teacher, she taught us about her religion and traditions, knowing full well we would never adopt them. As I grew older, I began to understand that my parents' mixed marriage and different religions proved that people are all very much alike; our differences are merely a matter of nuance. And although I love the sight and smell of the Christmas tree and the taste of the candies in an Easter basket, I know the Qur'an is the foundation of my life, the beauty of God at my fingertips. When I am in the States, I miss the melodic call to prayer that fills the air of Cairo five times a day.

As all who study it know, the Qur'an is far more than a collection of injunctions for following the straight path: it is a masterpiece of classical Arabic poetry and prose. Mohammed was illiterate, as were many of his companions; therefore, God intended the Qur'an to be as aesthetically moving as it is spiritually profound. I do not think there is an analogue in Western religion, but the Qur'an (which means literally "recitation") is meant to be spoken aloud, its audible beauty a part of its sacredness. The public recitation of its perfect rhythms, rhymes, and assonances is a revered art in the Islamic world. I have been a lifelong student of poetry, and much of my love of language, Arabic and English, stems from my contemplation of this most exquisite of texts.

From the moment I met Anwar Sadat, I knew he was a man of stalwart principles. I was young—only fifteen—and he was almost thirty, but I could sense that he personified all I had ever heard and been taught about the importance of strong character and even stronger faith. We came from two seemingly different worlds: I, from a middle-class family of Cairo; he, from a large, impoverished family from an equally impoverished village. What could we possibly have in common? How could we possibly hope to share a life? The answers are simple: at our core, we both, without doubt or question, loved God. Anwar could recite the verses of the Qur'an by heart, not simply because he had memorized them but also, and more important, because he lived by them. He had been tested in ways unimaginable to me. He had been in a prison where he lived in deplorable conditions. He had endured great physical discomfort and pain. I was young and idealistic when we met, but in reality, so was he. Anwar had ambitious dreams not just for himself, but also for his country and his people. His dreams took sustenance from his faith. In his autobiography, *In Search of Identity*, he wrote that God is everywhere, beneficent, compassionate, and merciful, and love is the means by which all things on this planet must relate: "If you have God for a friend, and establish a bond of mutual love between you, you will always have peace of mind whatever the circumstances." Being married to such a man was a blessing, though I cannot claim that I always viewed the world with such equanimity. In particular, I was always worried that Anwar would come to harm. He often said or did things with little regard for personal safety, and he mostly ignored my exhortations to be careful.

The attack on October 6, 1981 was not the first on my husband's life, though none had frightened him or caused him to take extra precautions such as wearing a bulletproof vest or increasing his security detail. He accepted that the length of his life was in the hands of God and no human being possessed the power to change what God has ordained. He was right, of course. Part of living is understanding that we are born to die. I accepted this, but I still worried about Anwar. Ironically, as much as I envisioned tragedy striking, I never imagined my life without Anwar. Trying to live after his death was something I could do only with the grace of God.

Not long ago I was sorting through the contents of my closet. Far back in a corner of one shelf in a space almost beyond my reach, I spied a small, dingy box held together with a frayed and faded blue ribbon. When I opened it, I discovered a cache of letters from Anwar, written early in our marriage when he and I were separated by his military duties. Here is the first letter he wrote to me following our marriage:

Jenny,

 I greet you and kiss you. This is the first time I write to you after our marriage and after you are bearing my name forever. This is why I am at a loss as to what I should write? Shall I say I love you, my dear beloved wife? If I say this, it will not suffice to express the reality of the sacred bond that united our hearts even before we saw each other. Then we became united and married, our souls united long before our marriage. I am writing to you now, my love, my hope, my inspiration, my happiness. So long as I live, I shall praise God, the mighty and beautiful, for what He has bestowed upon me. I shall pray to Him to guard you for me, kindness, sincerity, purity and strength of character and belief, chastity of soul, and depth of feelings and emotion.

Your husband

Looking again at his perfectly formed handwriting, hearing his words, I wept, for I realized again how blessed I have been. God did indeed bestow on us something wonderful. The Qur'an writes that the love between man and wife is a both a gift and reflection of God: "By another sign He created for you spouses from among yourselves, that you may live in peace with them and planted love and kindness in your heart. Surely there are signs in this for thinking men" (Qur'an, 30:21).

It was a sign for this woman as well. My husband, my four children, my grandchildren, and now my great-grandchildren were and are daily reminders of God's beneficence. Indeed, reverence for marriage and family are the heart of Islam. But pilgrimage, hajj, the fifth pillar of Islam, is the most sacred experience of any Muslim's life.

Ever since I was old enough to understand the meaning of the pilgrimage, I have dreamed of the day when I would go to Mecca to perform my hajj. It was my dream to be able to go while I was young enough and physically able to undertake, on my own power, the physical rigors of this fifth pillar of Islam. I have performed the lesser pilgrimage, the *umrah*, on more than one occasion, but never had I performed the hajj. During my family vacation in the summer of 1997, my heart told me that the next hajj would be my time. I wanted my children with me, if they felt the same. For any Muslim to undertake this holiest, most solemn journey for any other reason invalidates the pilgrimage and is against the spirit required of one performing hajj.

Each year during the holy month of hajj, the small Saudi Arabian city of Mecca, birthplace of the Prophet and forty years later the site of God's revelation of the Qur'an to him, is teeming with millions of pilgrims. Originally, the Sacred Mosque was not a large facility. Shortly after the death of the Prophet, the first expansion of the Sacred Mosque surrounding the Kaa'ba—the cube-shaped shrine built by Abraham and the focal point of the Sacred Mosque—began and has continued to some extent ever since. Today the Grand Mosque encompasses eighty-eight acres. The massive influx of pilgrims from so many different countries and cultures imposes severe physical demands on the local populations as well as the infrastructures of Mecca and Mina, the two primary sites of hajj that together cover only a mere ten square miles. Mina is important, because the Prophet Mohammed delivered his last sermon there. Both holy sites are located in a hot, rugged environment.

Caring for the needs of millions of people in such a small, inhospitable space would be an overwhelming task to most governments.

The Saudi Arabian government and the Saudi people, in the Muslim tradition of caring for guests to the best of one's ability, stretch themselves to great lengths and expense to secure the safety and well-being of the pilgrims. Because hajj is the opportunity for the Saudi nation to perform God's work, the government generously allocates billions of dollars to the development and maintenance of the holy sites of Mecca, Mina, and Medina. Medina is considered a holy city, because the Prophet and his followers escaped persecution from Meccans who were rejecting Islam in 622. Their escape is called the *hijrah*, and it marks the beginning of the Islamic calendar. When the Prophet and his followers arrived in Mina, the Prophet did not want to show any prejudice between those who had come with him and the people of Mina, so he allowed the selection of the location for the construction of his mosque to be determined by the whims of his camel. After dismounting, he left the animal free to wander. When his camel settled on the ground to rest, the Prophet moved toward him, made a mark on the sand, and announced that the will of God had been met. The mosque erected on that exact spot is where the Prophet prayed and was buried.

During my hajj, the temperatures in Mecca soared above 105 degrees. Hundreds of sprinklers had been installed along the paths of hajj to relieve the pilgrims; however, they did little to suppress the heat. Two and a half million people were living for days in this small space, yet the streets and facilities were never dirty. The government had trained hundreds and hundreds of people to speak different languages and understand different cultures. One of their primary duties was to assist lost or sick pilgrims twenty-four hours a day. Nothing, however, could have prepared me for the emotions I felt the moment I took my first step as a hajj pilgrim into the confines of the most sacred sanctuary of Islam. As I stepped slowly and effortlessly into the Grand Mosque, I was lifting my heart and soul in praise of God. Tears of joy were running down my face as I whispered my prayer of devotion. For the first time in my life, I felt as if every ounce of my being was completely at peace. First, I prayed for the health, happiness, and protection of my family, and I asked God to bless the soul of my husband. Then I raised my voice and heart in prayer for my friends. I cannot describe exactly how I was feeling, because I do not think human words can explain the ethereal nature of the calmness, the serenity, the closeness to God that embraced me. Together, with my oldest child, Loubna, on my arm, my children and I moved slowly in unison around the Kaa'ba. We were a tiny ship adrift on an ocean full of millions of other tiny ships, each being careful not to disturb the other as it circled seven times the place to which every Muslim in the world turns his eyes and heart in prayer. All around us was a vast, calm sea of pilgrims. To our sides were those who were physically unable to make it on their own. Instead of walking, they were being pushed in wheelchairs or carried on litters. Seeing their struggle made me feel immensely grateful that I was moving on my own. The millions of unique personalities were clothed similarly and moved together in a calm, quiet, and orderly manner, all of them moving deliberately in the same direction with the same purpose. We were millions yet one.

I was just a speck in that sea of humanity. I was completely aware that there were more than a million men and women and children from every society in the world feeling just as I was feeling. Their expressions, the looks in their eyes revealed the same awe, the same sense of deep reverence I was feeling. Husbands and wives were holding each other's hands. The faces of the sick and elderly radiated relief, tranquil in knowing that they were free of pain. My heart felt an all-consuming sense of peace and happiness. I was fulfilling my dream, my hajj, with my children by my side.

This is Islam. This is my religion.

Toward Peace

Peace in the Middle East has come to be regarded as something of an oxymoron, a pleasant but impossible aspiration, entertained by fantasists who might well believe that genies emerge from magic lamps. There is a widely shared perception that Arabs and Jews, whether by tradition, experience, or religious doctrine, are bound to hate each other, so efforts to resolve the conflicts that bedevil the Middle East are well-meaning but fruitless. I disagree, and I believe it is essential that both political leaders and regular people shift our thinking so that we regard the normalization of relations between Arabs and Israelis as not only achievable but also imperative. I am not so naive that I think such an effort will be easy, nor do I think that it will result in the eradication of terrorism, an end to the problems that plague the Holy Lands or universal human brotherhood: it is, however, a necessary first step to any of these goals—goals that are important in humanitarian and pragmatic terms.

I am too much a veteran of the world to be considered naive

and unrealistic. I know that peace between seemingly intractable foes can be made. I know because I have witnessed it. Attitudes can change. Now, the peace between Israel and Egypt is so well established as to be taken for granted, but this was not always the case. Egyptians and Israelis fought four wars in thirty years: we sent our sons and brothers and husbands to die in a testament to the differences between us. On each side, our triumphs—1967's Six-Day War for Israel, 1973's October War in Egypt—were moments of national euphoria, interpreted by the faithful as the hand of God, proof of our righteousness, and our defeats—1967 in Egypt, 1973 for Israel—were seen by some as divine punishment and plunged our people into crisis. We had learned to fear and to hate each other, to define ourselves in terms of our struggle against the other. When my husband decided to pursue peace with Israel, he was told it was impossible: the differences too great, the enmity too enduring. Furthermore, it was the wrong time: people would never accept it, and it could not last. But he did it because he believed it was right—and he believed that he could.

But before we go any further in examining how, as my husband quipped, politics can be "the art of the impossible," it is worth asking why we should bother to attempt it. What does this internecine conflict in faraway lands have to do with the rest of the world, and the United States in particular? Why is the United States called on to act as referee? The activist role the United States has played in the Middle East is a twentieth-century phenomenon and has been driven by a wide variety of considerations—some noble, others less so. These include the widespread horror of the Holocaust, the Cold War–era containment of communism, humanitarian principles, oil interests, the fight against terrorism, the effort to spread democracy, and scores of others. Today, despite challenges from rising economic powers elsewhere in the world, America is the only superpower. It therefore has significant influence on the world stage and has not hesitated to bring it to bear on issues central to its interests. And peace in the Middle East is unquestionably in America's interests. Since the latter half of the twentieth century, the Arab–Israeli conflict has been the most important lens through which Arabs view the West, and the United States in particular. This is true not only for Arabs in the Middle East but also much closer to home: A CAIR poll reports that "69 percent of American Muslims believe a just resolution to the Palestinian cause would improve America's standing in the Muslim world."

Since 9/11, America, which was accustomed to seeing itself as a beacon of hope and a force for good in the world—a perception that is not wrong but does not capture the whole story—has struggled with the question of "why they hate us." For while it is true that most Arabs and Muslims disavow terror, there is nevertheless a deep current of anti-American feeling in the Arab world. Arabs regard the United States' backing of Israel as blind and unquestioning, and they point to the dispossession of 4.5 million people, the number cited by the United Nations Relief and Works Agency (UNRWA); the fact that many Palestinians still live in crowded refugee camps under appalling conditions; and that those within the occupied territories are routinely denied basic civil and human rights while America not only looks on with utter complacency, but also appears to give unwavering support to the status quo.

Nothing illustrates this better than the 2008 Arab Opinion Poll conducted under the auspices of the University of Maryland's Sadat Chair for Peace and Development and Zogby International: 70 percent of Arabs polled reported having "no confidence" in the United States, and 95 percent reported that they perceived the United States as one of the two greatest threats they faced. Yet it is not, as some have posited, hatred for democracy (as we have seen, most Arabs voiced their support for democratic government), unqualified envy of Western lifestyles (Arabs for the most part are conservative and find many aspects of Western culture objectionable), or religious prejudice that underlies the discouraging numbers. The profound skepticism toward U.S. actions in the Middle East is generated by long-standing feelings of grievance, humiliation, and defiance, many of which can be traced back to the Arab-Israeli conflict.

The poll further reports that 86 percent of Arabs ranked Palestine as their "top issue" or "among the top three" in their priorities, an increase from the last five years, when 50 percent of Arabs polled said that the step that the United States could take that would most improve their view of it was brokering a comprehensive Middle East peace with Israeli withdrawal to the 1967 borders and establishing a Palestinian state with Jerusalem as its capital.

Throughout the broader Muslim world, in non-Arab countries like Pakistan, Indonesia, and Afghanistan, the Arab-Israeli conflict also carries a great deal of significance. Because Islam places such importance on the *ummah*, or the community of the faithful, Muslims are particularly attuned to the sufferings of their fellow Muslims, regardless of whether they share a common ethnicity. That this suffering takes place in lands sacred to Islam—Jerusalem, or Al-Quds in Arabic, is the third holiest city after Mecca and Medina—makes it all the more emblematic.

Having established the psychological importance of the Arab-Israeli struggle to the "hearts and minds" of Arabs and Muslims, I think it is useful to turn our attention to understanding what it is. It is my experience that even the best-informed and globally minded people often have little understanding of it, and such ignorance is both an effect and a cause of its reputation for incomprehensibility. People know it is hard to understand (much less solve) so they don't bother trying, and because they don't bother trying, they find it hard to understand. In his book *Palestine, Peace Not Apartheid*, former President Jimmy Carter identifies the root causes of the conflict as "occupation of Arab land, mistreatment of the Palestinians, and acceptance of Israel within its legal borders." This summary is a useful starting point and, I think, a good short answer. For a longer answer, one that addresses how these three things have acquired such political, emotional, and spiritual weight, I need to sketch a brief history of the precipitating events. There are numerous comprehensive histories of the struggle between Arabs and Israelis that provide a detailed analysis, but for this discussion, a basic overview is useful. Moreover, I will begin not in the ancient past, but in the century in which my own life has intersected these events and concentrate on the role Egypt has played.

In the wake of World War I and the defeat of the Turkish and German forces, the Ottoman Empire, which had controlled all of the Middle East, was divided, with much of the territory awarded to France and Britain. These two nations were charged with establishing "mandate" systems that would, ostensibly, instruct the locals in the art of self-governance. The French took control of what is now Syria and Lebanon, and the British were placed in charge of Iraq and Palestine (which included all of Jordan and Israel today). In Iraq they installed Prince Faisal, a Hashemite prince from Arabia, as king, and in 1932, Iraq became the first Arab mandate to gain independence. Meanwhile, Palestine was divided into two areas. In the territory east of the Jordan River, which they called the emirate of Transjordan, the British placed Abdullah Ibn Hussein, brother of King Faisal, on the throne. In the area to the west, Palestine, which lay between the Mediterranean and the west bank of the Jordan River, the British would rely first on a military government in Jerusalem, later a colonial governor, and above all, their skill as a "tutelary power." Theirs would be a disastrous tutorial.

The problems with colonial systems are many and well documented, and I have seen their painful legacy in Egypt and, indeed, throughout the rest of the world. In Palestine, the consequences were particularly bitter. British policy was poorly organized, contradictory, and deeply divisive, if not outright mendacious. In return for Arab participation in armed struggle against the Germans and the Turks (the "Arab rebellion" immortalized so memorably and inaccurately in the film *Lawrence of Arabia*), the British had promised the Arabs under Hussein, the sharif of Mecca (Faisal and Abdullah's father), self-rule and that the holy places would remain under the control of an independent, sovereign Muslim state. Meanwhile, in the oft-cited 1917 Balfour Declaration, made in a letter from British Foreign Secretary Arthur James Balfour to Lord Rothschild, the leader of the Zionist organization in Britain, which historian Arthur Goldschmidt, in *A Concise History of the Middle East*, calls the "Magna Carta of Zionism," the British also indicated their official support for allowing the Zionists to establish a "national home" in Palestine. Of course, the land in question was not uninhabited, and the Arab Palestinians, both Christian and Muslim, who had lived there for some thirteen hundred years, were not consulted. Although the declaration stated that it would not harm the civil and religious rights of the "existing non-Jewish communities," the document said nothing about their political rights, an omission with grave and persisting consequences.

With the British mandate established, significant numbers of Jewish immigrants began arriving from Europe. The Balfour Declaration had not initially been made public; nevertheless, rumors abounded, information was leaked, and Arab inhabitants could see the writing on the wall. Their anger and fear increased. The years between world wars were marked by revolts, riots, and general strikes. In the escalating violence, factions in both camps grew increasingly radicalized. British response alternated between heavy-handed tactics and utter passivity. As World War II loomed and even more Jews arrived, desperate to escape the growing fever of anti-Semitism in Europe, the British, bowing to Arab pressure, issued a white paper in 1939 that limited immigration to 15,000 a year. The Jewish population felt deeply betrayed, and militant Zionist groups like the Irgun and the Stern Gang carried out violent attacks on British installations in Palestine. Tragically, there were all too few places that Jews could go: the Western economies were recovering from the Great Depression, and many nations refused to allow the influx of refugees from the Third Reich in Germany. No one had imagined, however, what Hitler was planning.

In the wake of World War II, the white paper was eventually reversed, and particularly in the United States, the Zionist home-land was seen as a means of atoning for the Holocaust, whose magnitude was slowly being uncovered. In 1947, the British washed their hands of Palestine, which they called ungovernable: The mandate was given over to the fledgling United Nations, which voted to partition Palestine into Jewish, Arab, and (in the case of Jerusalem and its environs) international areas. Although it fell far short of their aspirations, the Zionists accepted this. The Arabs, who felt that they were being made to suffer for crimes in which they played no role, did not. Why should they have to make amends for the actions of the Germans? A Syrian delegate to the United Nations Special Committee on Palestine summarized the Arab position:

> The question of Palestine is altogether independent and sepa-rate from the question of persecuted persons of Europe. The Arabs of Palestine are not responsible in any way for the per-secution of the Jews in Europe. That persecution is con-demned by the whole civilized world, and the Arabs are among

**U.N. Partition Plan
1947**

Damascus
Mt. Hermon

LEBANON

SYRIA

Tyre

Zefat

Haifa

Sea of
Galilee

Nazareth

Mediterranean Sea

Irbid

Jenin

Netanya

Nablus

Jordan River

Tel Aviv

Ramallah

Amman

Jerusalem

Bethlehem

Gaza

Hebron

Dead
Sea

Rafah

Beersheba

El Arish

Al Karak

TRANSJORDAN

NEGEV

EGYPT

SINAI

☐ Jewish State
☐ Arab State
☐ International area

0   10   20   30 miles
0 10 20 30 40 kilometers

Eilat
Aqaba

*Gulf of
Aqaba*

SAUDI
ARABIA

those who sympathize with the persecuted Jews. However, the solution of that problem cannot be said to be a responsibility of Palestine, which is a tiny country and which had taken enough of those refugees and other people since 1920. . . . Any delegation which wishes to express its sympathy has more room in its country than has Palestine, and has better means of taking in these refugees and helping them.

There were terrorist acts on both sides, and even before the out-break of war, some 350,000 Palestinian Arabs fled the fighting. On May 14, 1948, just as the British mandate was set to expire—and the British had withdrawn far enough that they were unlikely to be involved in the fighting—Israel declared nationhood.

The next day, King Farouk of Egypt joined Syria, Lebanon, Iraq, and Transjordan in dispatching troops to prevent Zionist independence. The Arab forces were neither well prepared nor well coordinated. As a result, not only did Israel maintain its control over the areas assigned it by the United Nations partition plan, it seized part of the land assigned to the Palestinians. The other Palestinian territories—the West Bank and Gaza—were placed under the control of Jordan and Egypt, respectively. By the time the war was over, as many as 750,000 Arabs had been displaced. Approximately one-third fled to the West Bank, another third to the Gaza Strip, and the remainder to Jordan, Syria, and Lebanon. Most found shelter in hastily constructed refugee camps, where they awaited an opportunity to return to their homes. They wait still. To this day, the word that Arabs use to describe the 1948 defeat is *al-Nakba*—the disaster.

The armistice negotiated in 1949 did nothing to create a lasting peace; indeed, technically, Arab countries and Israel remained at war. Israel insisted on comprehensive settlement, including recognition of its statehood, which had been acknowledged by the

United States and Soviet Union immediately after its declaration. Arabs demanded that Israel withdraw to the portions of land allotted to them in the 1947 partition plan and allow the Arab Palestinians to return to their homes. The *Nakba* also set in motion political upheaval in the Arab world; the all-too-public-failure of the anciens régimes to resist the loss of Arab land contributed to their downfall. Within the next decade, leadership in many Arab states would be wrested from monarchs and princes, including Egypt.

In my teens at the time, I became deeply engaged, much more so than my peers, with understanding and following Egypt's independence movement. To be sure, the fire of freedom was burning within me, but in the years following the Palestine War, I was thinking more about Anwar Sadat. As I explain in my memoir, *A Woman of Egypt,* Anwar Sadat was my hero long before he was my husband. He was imprisoned for his continuing campaign against the British. His trial in 1948 made national headlines, and I followed the story breathlessly. When he was acquitted, I rejoiced—and soon after, at the home of my cousin, and much to my amazement, I came face-to-face with Anwar Sadat. It was love at first sight.

Shortly after our marriage in 1949, I went with him to his military post in Rafah, not far from the Gaza Strip. In Cairo, I had depended on the media for reportage about the Palestine War, but in Rafah, I could see for myself its ravages—the despair and dispossession of the Palestinian people, who were living in refugee camps hastily set up by UNRWA to provide Palestinians with basic necessities. Today, nearly sixty years later, UNRWA is still struggling to fulfill this mission, administering fifty-eight camps in Jordan, Lebanon, Syria, the West Bank, and the Gaza Strip that are home to 1.3 million registered refugees, a third of the total refugee population. The other two-thirds of the registered refugees live in and around the cities and towns of the host countries, and in the West

Israel
1949–67

Mediterranean Sea

LEBANON

Damascus

Mt. Hermon

Tyre

SYRIA

Zefat

Haifa

Sea of
Galilee

Nazareth

Irbid

Netanya

Jenin

Nablus

Jordan River

Tel Aviv

Ramallah

Amman

Jerusalem

JORDAN

Gaza Strip
(Egyptian
Administration)

Gaza

Hebron

Dead
Sea

Rafah

Beersheba

Al Karak

El Arish

ISRAEL

NEGEV

EGYPT

SINAI

- - - - - U.N. Approved
Boundary

0   10   20   30 miles
0 10 20 30 40 kilometers

Eilat

Aqaba

Gulf of
Aqaba

SAUDI
ARABIA

Bank and the Gaza Strip, often in the environs of official camps, but they too receive help from UNRWA. Then (and today as well), the conditions in which the refugees lived were cramped and squalid, with inadequate access to sewers, health care, and schools. Those early encounters with the camps made a lasting impression and helped me see the oft-invoked "plight of the Palestinians" not as an ideological or political problem but as a humanitarian crisis.

As I wrote at the start of this book, 1952 was a momentous year for Egypt, for it was the year that the Free Officers won our independence. The Free Officers, one of whom was my husband, were not a political party, but rather a group of nine young Egyptian Army officers who planned and executed this historic and bloodless military coup d'état. In 1954, Gamal Abdel Nasser, the leader of the coup, assumed leadership of the nation. Over the next sixteen years, he loomed large on the world stage. His ambitions were sweeping: dismantle the ancien régime and remake the nation according to egalitarian, socialist ideals. In 1954, he also signed an evacuation agreement with the British, an act that placed Suez under Egyptian authority, thereby removing all vestiges of colonial rule.

The domestic agenda was not Nasser's only concern. Two events underlined the already acrimonious relationship with Egypt's newly formed neighbor to the east. In 1954, the Lavon affair (named for the Israeli minister of defense, Pinhas Lavon, who resigned as a result) was uncovered: a plot hatched by the Israeli secret service to blow up British and American targets in Egypt, blame Nasser, and ultimately derail the pullout from the Suez Canal. The ring was discovered, creating a climate of suspicion and hostility toward both Israel and, sadly, Egyptian Jewry. The second event was an Israeli raid on Gaza (which was, in the wake of the 1948 war, under Egyptian administrative control). This made Nasser painfully aware of Egypt's need for weapons, since the army was using the same outmoded arms that had failed so miserably in the war in Palestine. He looked first to the United States and the United Kingdom, but he would not agree to their preconditions, one of which was joining the Baghdad Pact, a U.K.-led mutual defense treaty with Pakistan, Turkey, Iran, and Iraq. Not only did he refuse, but he also persuaded Jordan and Lebanon not to join either. Nasser then turned to the Soviet Union. In response, the United States withdrew its pledge of funding for the Aswan High Dam, a project essential to Egypt's future. The Soviet Union stepped in, but Nasser, furious with the United States, nationalized the Suez Canal Company, an act seen as the Arab world standing up to the Western powers, an image that grew only more exalted after the Suez crisis—or the War of Tripartite Aggression, as it was known in Egypt—that was to follow. Britain devised a secret plot with France and Israel to regain the canal by force. The plan was carried out beginning October 29, 1956. Suddenly our newly independent country was under siege from two of the most powerful nations in the world and Israel, whose very existence had come to symbolize injustice toward Arabs. The British and French strafed our cities with air fire while the Israelis invaded Sinai.

The Soviet Union condemned the aggression and, in a rare moment of agreement between the superpowers, so did the United States. Through the offices of the United Nations, both nations called for immediate withdrawal. The international waterways would remain open to Israeli ships and Israel would withdraw its troops from Sinai. Three months later, Israel did, though practicing a scorched-earth policy along the way. A United Nations peacekeeping force was stationed in Sinai, where it would remain until the eve of the 1967 war.

In addition to giving my young children and me nightmares, the War of Tripartite Aggression prompted Nasser to expel British and French citizens living in Egypt (we were at war with their countries), nationalize what were once their businesses, and pave the way for the eventual socialist-inspired nationalization of the economy. In short order, the Jewish population and almost all other foreign communities packed up and left.

Nasser, meanwhile, had transformed a military defeat into a political victory. He was a hero of the grandest proportions throughout the Arab world. So dazzling was his aura that in 1958, Syria merged with Egypt into a single nation, the United Arab Republic, a republic that lasted, however, a mere three years. Palestinians in particular found Nasser's belief in Arab unity and concomitant defiance of the West heroic. And indeed, Nasser played a role in forming the Palestine Liberation Organization (PLO), which was created during the first Arab summit in 1964 in order to provide centralized leadership to the nation in exile.

Everything changed when the Arab world lost the Six-Day War. In 1967, Israel attacked a Jordanian village that it alleged was a base for the PLO. Syrian and Israeli planes skirmished. Because we shared a common defense pact with Syria, Egypt too began preparing for war. The Soviet Union informed Nasser that Israel was massing troops on the Syrian border, whereupon Nasser sent 100,000 troops across Sinai to the Israeli border. It is nevertheless unclear whether Nasser truly wanted war. Eager to end the goading from fellow Arab leaders that he was "hiding behind UN peacekeepers" and allowing Israeli ships to pass through the straits of Tiran, and determined to maintain his prestige in the Arab world, he ordered the UN peacekeepers to leave Sinai, which they did, and then he closed the straits of Tiran.

Still, Nasser hoped for mediation. The U.S. State Department was trying to broker peace while assuring us that Israel was also pursuing diplomatic means to end the conflict. Two days later, however, the Israelis attacked. Over the next six days, which from then on would be known as the *Naksa*, or setback in Arabic, Israel took control of Sinai, including the Suez Canal, Gaza, the West Bank, the Golan Heights, and the Old City of Jerusalem. It now controlled more than three times the amount of land it had prior to the war. Fifteen thousand Egyptian soldiers had been killed. The consequences for the Palestinians were severe. According to a UN report, *The Origins and Evolution of the Palestine Problem*:

> The great majority of Palestinians in the West Bank and Gaza were made refugees—many for the second time, having sought refuge in these areas during the first exodus of 1948. Those that stayed in Israeli-occupied territory after 1967 came to form a new category distinct from those within Israel's pre-1967 borders, who were entitled to Israeli citizenship. This new class was one of a people under foreign military occupation, subject to military rule, its repercussions and its consequences for the suppression of civil liberties and rights.
>
> But both the Palestinians inside Israel's pre-1967 borders and those in the occupied territories accounted for a minority of the Palestinian people. The majority were now in total exile. In June 1967, of about 2.7 million persons of Palestinian origin, about 1.7 lived in Israel or the occupied territories—about 1 million in the West Bank, 400,000 in the Gaza Strip and 300,000 in the areas controlled by Israel. As a result of the 1967 war, almost half a million fled their homes, leaving about 900,000 Palestinians in the areas newly occupied by Israel, a total of 1.2 million under Israeli control. One million five hundred thousand were refugees in exile—in countries other than their own, their homeland under the control of the Jewish State.

The spiritual and psychological effects of the *Naksa* were enormous: Arab nations were shamed; Israel appeared invincible.

The pan-Arab movement was abandoned. Likewise, the Israeli victory fortified the belief of many Jews that God was on their side. In addition, Egypt lost two major sources of revenue, the oil wells in Sinai and the Suez Canal, in one blow. Indeed, Israel's territorial gains were problematic even for the Israelis. What would they do with these new lands? How would they deal with the people whose lives they now controlled? Israel was in flagrant violation of international law, for it was no longer permissible to annex lands seized by military conquest. In the months following the war, the international community repeatedly called for the return of areas seized by Israel. In November 1967, the UN Security Council passed Resolution 242, which has been central to all discussions of Middle East peace that have followed. It called for a withdrawal of Israeli armed forces from territories occupied in the recent conflict, recognition of every state in the region, free navigation through international waterways, and a just settlement of the Palestinian refugee problem; and it established demilitarized zones and a special representative appointed by the United Nations. Although both sides accepted what has come to be known as a "land-for-peace formula," it was never implemented.

Indeed, the mood was far from conciliatory. In August 1967, the Arab leaders convened in Khartoum and announced the "Three Nos": no peace, no recognition of Israel, and no negotiation with Israel. August 1967 saw the start of the undeclared "war of attrition" between Egypt and Israel—six years of skirmishes in the Canal Zone, Upper Egypt, and Cairo. The Israelis pounded our cities of Suez, Ismailia, and Port Said, while Egypt fought back against the Bar Lev Line, a chain of fortifications the Israelis were building along the eastern edge of the canal. The Israelis launched air raids at industrial and even civilian targets.

The aftermath of the 1967 war was a watershed moment for me personally as well. I was volunteering at the Red Crescent with the wounded. The injuries were hideous—men blinded, maimed, crippled, missing arms and legs—and for each injury I could see, I knew there were scores more I could not. It was clear that these men who had given so much for their country would return to very bleak prospects and that most could not hope to return to the lives they had led before being wounded. Soon after the war, I was instrumental in the construction of the Wafa 'wal Amal, a rehabilitation center for injured veterans. In 1967, looking at the rows upon rows of war wounded, I knew where my allegiance lay: with peace.

Meanwhile, the Palestinians, seeing the failure of the Arab armies—and indeed, the rest of the world—to end their dispossession, began taking matters into their own hands. Guerrilla groups launched campaigns of violence against the Israeli occupiers, while the Israelis exacted severe reprisals in a pattern that would become all too familiar. In 1968 the PLO adopted a new charter committing all Palestinians to continue the fight to liberate their homeland, while calling Israel "entirely illegal." Israel refused to deal with the PLO at all. In 1969, Yasir Arafat, head of the guerrilla group Fatah, assumed leadership of the PLO, and the Palestinian national identity was officially recognized by the United Nations. A year later, in 1970, Arafat and other members of the Palestinian leadership would accuse Nasser of abandoning their cause when he agreed to the U.S.-sponsored Rogers plan, which called for Israel's unilateral withdrawal to pre-1967 borders but signaled Nasser's willingness to pursue a negotiated settlement. (The Rogers plan never amounted to anything; Israel vetoed it.) By September, thereafter referred to as Black September, the Palestinian leadership would be engaged in a bloody civil war against the forces of Jordan's King Hussein.

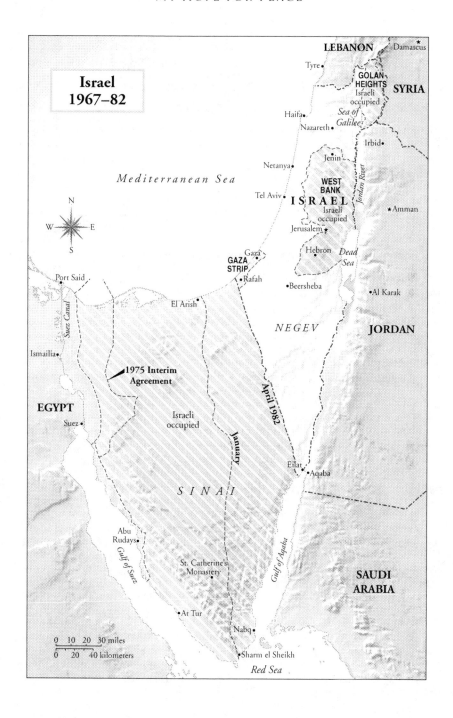

Israel
1967–82

LEBANON   Damascus
          Tyre
                    GOLAN
                    HEIGHTS   SYRIA
                    Israeli
                    occupied
Haifa   Sea of
     Nazareth   Galilee
                         Irbid
Netanya   Jenin
                         Jordan River
     Tel Aviv   WEST
            BANK
Mediterranean Sea   ISRAEL   Amman
            Israeli
            occupied
     Jerusalem

N   Gaza
W   E   GAZA   Hebron   Dead
S   STRIP   Sea
          Rafah
Port Said   Beersheba
                         Al Karak
El Arish
               NEGEV   JORDAN
Ismailia

1975 Interim
Agreement
          April 1982
EGYPT   Israeli
Suez   occupied
          January
                    Eilat
                         Aqaba
          S I N A I

Abu
Rudays   Gulf of Aqaba
     Gulf of Suez
          St. Catherine's   SAUDI
            Monastery   ARABIA

     At Tur
               Nabq
0 10 20 30 miles   Sharm el Sheikh
0   20   40 kilometers   Red Sea

The tension between the monarch and the Palestinian state-within-a-state had been building. After the 1967 war, an additional 200,000 Palestinians had fled to Jordan, bringing the population of Palestinians to over half a million. Militant groups were using Jordan as a staging ground for attacks on Israel, including a series of spectacular hijackings, and Jordan had been feeling the brunt of the Israeli retaliation. The more militant Palestinian leadership chafed under Hussein and finally mounted an insurrection against him. Hussein responded by sending troops into Amman, where, after vicious fighting, Hussein prevailed, forcing the PLO to flee Jordan for Beirut, which would become a new base for the fight against Israel. The presence and influence of the PLO in Lebanese politics would become one of the precipitating factors in the Lebanese civil war. Driving the PLO from Lebanon was the justification for Israel's 1982 invasion of that country and subsequent occupation of southern Lebanon. Thereafter, the PLO would set up its headquarters in Tunis.

But in the fall of 1970, those events were still far off, and Nasser, who had been an ardent spokesperson for the Palestinian cause, convened a peace conference in Cairo in an attempt to broker an end to the terrible conflict between King Hussein and the PLO. The effort literally killed him. Already in poor health, having developed diabetes and a heart problem, he died in September 1970 at the age of fifty-two, the victim of a sudden heart attack. Anwar and I, like millions of others, were overcome with grief. Abdel Nasser had been a friend, an Egyptian patriot, and a hero to the Arabs.

Thus, it was a nation in mourning that elected Anwar Sadat to the presidency on October 15 of that year. In addition, Egypt was nearly bankrupted by war, partially occupied by Israel, engaged in a fierce undeclared war, and allied with the Soviet Union, a world power that had proven time and time again to be unreliable. By

1971, Sadat, with his own vision for Egypt—one that was at odds with the socialist program initiated under Nasser—had outmaneuvered his opponents and consolidated his authority. He was ready to implement a fourfold campaign to transform Egypt into a modern nation. First, he began laying the groundwork for democracy: he eased restrictions on the press, allowed religious organizations to demonstrate in the universities, freed the political prisoners, lifted the decrees that put private property under government custodianship, lifted the ban on international travel, and established a multiparty system. Second, he opened Egypt to foreign investment and industry and, conversely, encouraged Egyptians to go abroad to seek out employment opportunities, since the Egyptianization of the economy had destroyed the private sector. Third, he shifted the strategic orientation of the country from the Soviet Union to the United States, which he correctly assessed would come to be the sole superpower. Indeed, in an interview with journalist Ahmed Bahaa el Din some eighteen years before the collapse of communism, Anwar posed his own question to the journalist. My husband asked el Din to identify the major powers in the world. He replied, not surprisingly, the Soviet Union and the United States. Anwar responded with a familiar Egyptian expression: "Let me tell you something that you can wear as an earring. There is only one power in the world: the USA." Finally, and most important, he wanted to make peace with Israel: our nation was tired of bloodshed, tired of seeing the money that could have been spent on badly needed development projects being funneled toward defense.

Sadat was serious about peace. On the day of President Nasser's funeral, Anwar sent a message to President Nixon through the United States envoy, Elliott Richardson. He said, and these were his exact words: "Tell President Nixon that I am ready for peace." Anwar waited but received no reply from the U.S. government.

Because of the Cold War and our defeat in the 1967 war, no government, least of all that of the United States, was willing to take what came out of Egypt very seriously. "We Arabs are always talking, talking, talking about what we will do, but then we do nothing. No wonder no one believes us," Anwar often remarked.

As his overtures for peace were ignored, Sadat and the Arabs began preparing for war. My husband warned the international community repeatedly that military action was inevitable, but few took heed. Nor did they regard the Arab armies as much of a threat, for not only had they been crushed in 1967, but Egypt's relationship with its most powerful strategic partner, the Soviet Union, was severely strained. In 1972, Sadat had expelled the Russian military advisers; he was tired of their false promises and their failure to deliver, and he was eager to free Egypt from the Soviet social and economic influence. But these same pundits who dismissed my husband's warnings as empty threats were mistaken: they did not grasp the impossibility of the Arab situation. Although we were not at war, we were not at peace; there were armed clashes and air attacks, and the military was always on high alert without actually being deployed. In addition, the Israelis were establishing settlements, creating "facts on the ground" in the territories seized in the 1967 war: the West Bank, East Jerusalem, the Golan Heights, and, most painful for Egypt, our own Sinai. Such building campaigns seemed to announce Israel's intention never to part with Jordanian, Palestinian, Syrian, and Egyptian lands.

On October 6, 1973, the forces of Egypt and Syria mounted a surprise air and artillery assault, overwhelming the defensive Bar Lev Line on the eastern bank of the Suez, a fortification that the Soviets had said only an atom bomb could breach. Simultaneously, Syrian forces attacked Israeli troops in the Golan Heights. Soon the Suez Canal was back in Egyptian hands. The Arabs were winning—indeed, a contingent of Israeli military was pinned down and trapped by Egyptian forces. It was at that point that America intervened. Although Egypt had help from the Soviet Union, the shah of Iran, and the eleven oil-producing states that, for the first time, imposed an oil embargo on America, my husband had no desire to fight against the United States—nor did he wish to spark a nuclear confrontation between the superpowers. For the only time in history, all U.S. forces had been placed on high alert. January 1974 witnessed the first agreement on the disengagement of Egyptian and Israeli forces. Brokered by Henry Kissinger, it provided for Egypt to reoccupy the east bank of the canal (and thus regain control over it) and Israel to withdraw from the other bank.

Yet the consequences of the October war transcended the terms of the uneasy peace that concluded it. That victory restored Arab pride, destroyed the myth of Israeli invincibility, and allowed Anwar to negotiate an end to conflict from a position of strength and credibility. A scant four years later, the president of Egypt would step onto a red carpet in Tel Aviv. Anwar Sadat, the leader political pundits had predicted would not hold office for more than a few months, had done the unthinkable: he was coming to the house of his enemy to speak of peace. I knew my husband would take bold steps, though I never imagined he would take his case directly to the Israelis. But he had had enough of intermediaries, and in a speech to the opening session of the Egyptian Parliament on November 9, 1977, he announced his intention "to travel to the ends of the earth if this will in any way protect any Egyptian boy, soldier or officer from being killed or wounded. . . . I am ready to go to their country, even to the Knesset itself, and talk with them."

On November 15, Israeli Prime Minister Menachem Begin extended a formal invitation, and Anwar accepted. And so it was on November 20, on the first day of the Eid al-Adha, one of Islam's most important religious feasts, that Anwar performed his morning prayers at the Al-Aqsa Mosque, the third holiest shrine in Islam; visited the Haram al-Sharif, or the Dome of the Rock, from where we believe the Prophet ascended into heaven on his night journey; and finally, stood before the Israeli Knesset, where he was greeted with a standing ovation. The significance of this occasion cannot be overstated. To say it was a grand gesture is to belittle it. Until that moment, no Arab leader had recognized Israel's right to exist, much less set foot on Israeli soil. There were many who said to my husband, "It is not the right time. You cannot make peace with the Israelis." Yasir Arafat and Syria's Hafez Assad considered Anwar's move toward peace a betrayal. George Habash, leader of the Popular Front for the Liberation of Palestine (PFLP), openly called for the assassination of Anwar Sadat, describing his visit to Israel as the greatest crime in the history of the Arab people since the creation of the State of Israel.

Egyptian embassies in various nations were attacked, and a newspaper editor—a close friend of Anwar's who had accompanied him to Jerusalem—was assassinated in Cyprus. And it was not only the Palestinians who objected: Muammar Gadhafi of Libya broke relations the moment Anwar's plane touched down on Israeli soil. Syria, Iraq, South Yemen, Algeria, and the PLO boycotted the peace talks Anwar convened at Cairo's Mena House hotel in December 1977 and held their own summit in Tripoli, where they too decided to sever relations.

A year later, after the signing of the Camp David Accords, Egypt was cast out of the Arab League, and the league's headquarters were moved from Cairo to Tunis. Egypt was being punished: all Arab aid was stopped, a devastating blow that left our economy, which is considerably less wealthy than those of the oil-rich Gulf nations, in shambles.

In 1979, Anwar was dismayed, yet confident that the Arabs would come back to Egypt. Egypt is the largest and most populous of the Arab states. Today, one out of every three Arabs is Egyptian, and in addition to our leadership role in regional politics, Egypt is the cultural capital of the Arab world. Our newspapers boast the largest circulations, our centers of higher education are many and influential—in particular, Al-Azhar, the world's oldest university and the seat of Sunni learning. Egyptian literature, cinema, and music are exported throughout the Arabic-speaking nations from Morocco to Yemen. No, Egypt's isolation would not be permanent, and Anwar predicted, "It will take the Arabs no less than ten years to realize the impact of what I have done. And by then, they will not get half of what they could have if they had joined us at the Mena House [Cairo] meeting or Camp David." Anwar's words have proven prophetic: the Palestinians and the Arabs did take more than ten years to accept, and adopt, his way of thinking, although not his method of making peace. Sadly, they will be lucky if they get a fraction of what Sadat was offering to bring them in 1977.

It still strikes me as a bitter irony that the Palestinians were so categorical and acrimonious in their rejection of his efforts. As Sadat's speech, and indeed, every action that followed demonstrated, he believed that justice for the Palestinians was an essential prerequisite for peace in the Middle East. When he addressed the Knesset in November 1977, Anwar laid out in detail his five points for peace:

1. An end to the occupation of all Arab land occupied after the 1967 war.
2. The achievement of the fundamental rights of the Palestinian people, which includes their right of self-determination and the establishment of their own state.

3. The right of all states in the region to live safely and securely within their borders.
4. The acceptance of the principles of the United Nations Charter, particularly those concerning the absence of force as a means of resolving differences.
5. An end to the state of belligerence in the region.

Not once did my husband presume to be the representative of the Palestinians, yet he understood that he could not bring a comprehensive peace to the region without the participation of the Palestinians. Never, not for one moment, did he betray the Palestinian people or their cause. In Jerusalem, he told the Israelis and the whole world that a peace based on the occupation of the land of others is not a serious peace, and certainly not a fair and lasting one. He remained loyal to these concerns in his negotiations for peace at Camp David.

The Camp David talks, which took place between September 5 and 17, 1978, at the presidential retreat in the hills of Maryland, were convened at the invitation of President Jimmy Carter. Sadat's trip to Jerusalem had been a quantum leap forward toward peace, but the work of hammering out actual details of any possible settlements was yet to be done. Carter hoped that the privacy and peace of Camp David would prove conducive to continuing the momentum that my husband had created. Begin, Sadat, and Carter, together with their closest advisers, participated in round after round of intense sessions. Neither the Palestinians, nor any other Arab government, would attend. However, contrary to some Arab claims, the purpose of the Camp David meeting was not about establishing "a separate peace" by which Egypt alone might benefit. On the contrary, the framework of the Camp David Accords states: "Egypt, Israel, Jordan, and the representatives of the Palestinian people should participate in negotiations on the resolution of the Palestinian problem in all its aspects." Menachem Begin approved of this, but by then, perhaps Palestinian opposition was too fevered and too entrenched to reconsider its position, much less actually examine the accords. As naive as this sounds, I do wonder whether the most vociferous rejectionists even bothered to read the text. I am reminded of a reception in Bonn that was given in honor of an Egyptian diplomat returning home from Camp David: the guest list included international media correspondents and diplomats, one of whom was the PLO representative. Everyone was eager to hear firsthand about what had transpired at Camp David, and our official was happy to comply. In the middle of his description, the Palestinian interrupted: "I'm sorry. I must leave now before you convince me of the value of Camp David!" Surprised, the Egyptian official replied, "Why shouldn't I convince you? You know . . ." and before he could finish his statement, the PLO representative walked away.

Specifically, two agreements emerged from those historic days in September. The first, A Framework for Peace in the Middle East, proposed a five-year transitional period in the West Bank and Gaza during which Israeli forces would be withdrawn and replaced by an elected, fully autonomous, and self-governing authority. This was not the creation of a Palestinian state, but it was an essential first step, or springboard, to that end. It gave Palestinians the right to participate in the determination of their own future, in negotiations to resolve the final status of the West Bank and Gaza, and then to produce an Israeli-Jordanian peace treaty. Furthermore, it reaffirmed both parties' commitment to Resolution 242, which prohibits the acquisition of land by force and calls for Israeli withdrawal to pre-1967 borders, and secure, recognized borders for all the nations. It also invited the participation of other Arab governments.

The second document, Framework for the Conclusion of a Peace Treaty Between Egypt and Israel, provided for the full withdrawal of Israeli forces from Sinai, the dismantling of Israeli settlements there, and the establishment of normal, peaceful relations between the two countries to be formalized in a permanent treaty. The initialing ceremony, held in the East Room of the White House, was cause for celebration to be sure, but there was still considerable work to be done to reach a permanent treaty between Egypt and Israel—and the world has yet to implement the text of the Framework for Peace in the Middle East.

Many books have been written about the Camp David meetings, so I shall leave the play-by-play descriptions to historians and participants, but suffice it to say that a game of wits, if I may call it so, was played out at Camp David between Menachem Begin and Anwar Sadat, with Jimmy Carter acting as an honest broker, trying to maintain equilibrium between the two. Begin wanted to analyze and debate every detail. Sadat, meanwhile, wanted to discuss and agree on the general issues and leave the details for his ministers. My husband was negotiating not only for Egypt, but also for all Arabs—exactly as he had proclaimed he would during his speech in Jerusalem. Anwar wanted an agreement on peace, not a long list of requirements and conditions that had to be met in advance. For all their obvious differences, the Israeli prime minister and the Egyptian president were also curiously alike: both had fought against British occupation of their countries, sacrificed mightily for independence, and spent time in prison and labor camps for their cause. Both were courageous leaders, patriots, and soldiers who had waged wars long before each began to work together for peace.

I shall always be sorry that I was unable to be with Anwar in Maryland during that historic time. Aliza Begin had accompanied her husband, and Rosalynn Carter had also invited me. Instead I went to Paris to be with my daughter and grandson, where he was receiving treatment for severe asthma. Anwar and I were in close contact by phone, however. I shall never forget the day—only two days after he had told me he was leaving Camp David because the talks were fruitless, and I begged him to reconsider—that he reported that he and Begin had come to terms.

On November 10, 1978, Anwar Sadat and Menachem Begin were jointly awarded the Nobel Peace Prize. It was the first time the prize had been granted to laureates from the Middle East, and it was a shining moment, a vindication of all that my husband stood for. Because Begin was not dismantling settlements in Palestine and had actually announced plans to expand them, Anwar would not attend the ceremonies. And he gave the prize money to his home village of Mit Abul Kum. In his account of the Camp David Accords, *The Blood of Abraham*, Jimmy Carter writes, "Perhaps the most serious omission of the talks was not clarifying in writing Begin's promise concerning the settlement freeze during the subsequent peace talks." The issue of these settlements, in the West Bank especially, continues to be one of the most contentious and divisive in the Arab-Israeli conflict.

On March 26, 1979, at the signing ceremony for the Egyptian-Israeli Treaty held on the South Lawn of the White House, these three men made history. To behold so many men and women who had spent so much of their lives waging war against each other, shaking hands, breaking bread, and reimagining a wholly different kind of future was indescribably moving. The signing of the treaty was a watershed moment in the history of the Middle East—and not because all the problems were going to disappear. They did not. The Camp David Accords had two parts, and the treaty between Israel and Egypt was the realization of only half of them. Nor did Anwar, who staked so much on this treaty, imagine that this single agreement could be a cure-all. It was, however, a potent demonstration of the fact that the barriers of history and hatred are not insuperable. The peace made that day has endured for thirty years, and cold as it may sometimes appear, it has had a stabilizing effect on the region; by averting another bloody, pointless war, it has spared the lives of countless souls.

On a personal note, it was not until after 1979 that I was able to gain a true appreciation of Israel as something other than an adversary. My experiences since then have allowed me to develop some insight into the Jewish state—its goals and positions, its aspirations and fears—and the inaccuracy of equating Israeli public opinion with hard-line positions. I have seen the depth and passion of its peace movements, the multiplicity and vigor of its civil society, and even in the darkest of moments of conflict between Arabs and Israelis, I know that the headlines in Washington and Cairo do not tell the whole story.

Peace has also enabled Egypt to reorient itself toward improving the lot of the average Egyptian, strengthening our economy, and husbanding our resources. Education, health care, and infrastructure are necessarily neglected in times of war. The idea that war is a barrier to development seems to me quite basic, so I could never quite understand those Egyptians, in particular some secular intellectuals, who categorically rejected Sadat's peace. Now, however, many of these same people have changed their tunes. One in particular is Saad El-Din Ibrahim, a professor of sociology at the American University in Cairo, director of the Arab Affairs Unit at the Al-Ahram Center for Political and Strategic Studies, and author of numerous books in Arabic and English. Unlike most other opponents, who were histrionic in their complaints, he presented his disagreement from an analytical, scientific approach. Anwar and I were not unaware of his opposition. We knew there would be many who disagreed with peace with Israel and the actions my husband took to support it. Believing, however, that the most advantageous way to deal with criticism was to engage our critics in discussion, I invited Dr. Ibrahim to talk with my husband in our home in Alexandria during the summer of 1981. This was not such an unusual step; Anwar routinely held face-to-face meetings with professors and other intellectuals who opposed his policies. He wanted to talk with them informally, apart from the trappings of state—not to try to persuade his opponents, but rather to hear and debate for himself their differing viewpoints. Dr. Ibrahim and Anwar, who were miles apart in their opinions, spent three stormy hours mapping that distance. When I interrupted to bring them to the table for lunch, I whispered to Dr. Ibrahim that the president was not angry with him. That was not Anwar's style; he never took disagreement as a personal attack. On the contrary, passionate debate was the vehicle Anwar used to search out a common ground with those who did not understand the motives and objectives of his policies and decisions.

Sixteen years later, in 1995, Dr. Ibrahim submitted a research memorandum, "The Vindication of Sadat in the Arab World," to a seminar of Middle Eastern scholars in Washington. Once severely critical of Sadat and his politics, he concluded that the Arab world had begun to revise its image of President Sadat: "To be sure, the man still has many sharp critics. But even these would grudgingly concede that Sadat was a commendable Arab leader and a states-man; that in many ways he was ahead of his time."

Not too many years ago, the Professor's World Peace Academy organized a conference, The Sadat Peace Initiative: A Scholarly Appraisal. Professors from Egypt, Israel, and the United States submitted position papers for consideration and debate. Abdel-Aziz Nawar and Abdel-Karim el-Ahwal, both original supporters of my husband's peace initiative, participated in the conference, as did other Egyptian professors who initially had been opposed to his stance. Participation of the latter is, in itself, proof that Sadat's opponents have come around to accepting and backing his actions for peace in the Middle East. One particular paper, "A Socio-Cultural Account of the Sadat Peace Initiative," authored by Dr. el-Ahwal of the Institute of Planning in Cairo, impressed me. He wrote that there is a newly born peace generation who believes, as Sadat believed, that war means "destruction, agony, problems, and human suffering." Egypt has no shortage of problems, but to grow up in a nation without war is a powerful thing, and it is my hope that these "peace generations" will not only safeguard, but also share the blessing of peace.

Although I have lived long enough to see the tide of Arab opinion regarding my husband change, the shift has been gradual, and his death was not the impetus for the reversal. On the contrary, the chorus of condemnation grew only more insistent and the attacks more vicious in the aftermath of his assassination. I found this particularly demoralizing, because Islam instructs us to put aside all differences and remove any anger we may feel in our hearts for those who have passed away. The Palestinian leader Salah Khalaf gloated and publicly pronounced: "Opening fire on Sadat opens fire on the ugliest era in Arab history." Another, Nayef Hawatima, described Sadat's assassination as "the gateway to the elimination of the conflict and the return of revolutionary Egypt to the front line against Zionism and American imperialism." Yasir Arafat lauded and congratulated the murderers of the traitor Anwar Sadat in one of his speeches: "This operation carried out by the great Egyptian people, proves that they could not have pardoned the one who relinquished Jerusalem and who struck the Palestinian cause and extended his hand to sign the treacherous Camp David plot against the Palestinian people and the Arab Nation. This is the message of the army and the people of Abdel Nasser." There were celebrations in the Palestinian neighborhoods of Beirut.

These outpourings of hate from the Palestinians were hard to bear; harder still was the smear campaign undertaken by some members of the Egyptian and Arab press. Perhaps they hoped to dismantle Anwar's peace by discrediting him—and his family—personally. Anwar was accused of being a Zionist agent, a toady to the West, an infidel. Rumors circulated that I had stolen works of art from an Egyptian museum, that I dispatched a helicopter to fetch my groceries each morning, that Anwar and I owned twelve houses in Cairo and properties all over the world. Cairo's newspapers added credibility to the rumors by printing these false accusations in the most prominent spots. One professor wrote an article saying he had been pressured into awarding my son his engineering degree. He added, "Jehan Sadat's master's degree is also fake." That the charges were lies, sometimes ridiculous lies at that, did not make them less repeated, or less painful. I was accustomed to these personal attacks, but to see my children slandered in print was excruciating, since Anwar and I had been assiduous in our efforts to shelter them from the public eye. The smear campaign forced me to step down from running the nonprofit organizations that I had begun: the Wafa 'wal Amal, the SOS Children's Village for orphaned children, and the Talla Society women's collective.

I struggled to remind my children and myself that the vituperative press campaign was demonstration of the Arabic saying, "Whoever achieves great things has many enemies." Time has proved a balm, not only because it softens the edges of painful memories, but also because one after the other, events in the region have borne out the acuity of Sadat's vision.

The civil strife in Lebanon exposed just how little the nations of the rejectionist front—Syria, Iraq, and Libya—were willing to go in order to protect the interests of the Palestinians on whom they had lavished so much rhetoric. The PLO had been forced to relocate its headquarters to Beirut following the events of Black September in Jordan in 1970. Its presence further challenged the fragile relationship among political and religious groups in Lebanon, including Sunnis, Shiites, Maronite Christians, and Druze, each of which maintained armed militias. Since the civil war started in 1975, the nation had been embroiled in periodic violence. As home to a new Palestinian state within a state, it also became the staging ground for Palestinian attacks on Israel, and thus a target for Israel's reprisals.

In 1982, Israel invaded Lebanon. As a consequence, the PLO was driven from Lebanon. Yasir Arafat and his administration were granted safe passage out of the city, overseen by British, French, and American peacekeeping troops. In the wake of these departures— the peacekeepers withdrew soon after the Palestinian leadership decamped—terrible bloodshed ensued. The world was horrified by the massacres of hundreds of Palestinians at the Sabra and Shatila refugee camps. Although Christian Phalanges did the actual killing, Israeli forces oversaw the action. Indeed, an Israeli inquiry into the atrocity found that General Ariel Sharon had facilitated the massacre and made (the evidently nonbinding) recommendation that he be excluded from future cabinets. In any event, Israeli troops would remain in south Lebanon until 2000.

During the 1982 invasion of Lebanon, Iraq and Libya did nothing to help the embattled Lebanese or Palestinians, and when the PLO attempted to establish headquarters in Tripoli, it was Syria's Hafez Assad who prevented it. In 1983, disgusted with the anti-Palestinian countries and forced by Syria to leave Lebanon, Arafat was received in Egypt (en route to Tunis), where he found an Egyptian public perfectly comfortable supporting the Palestinian cause while remaining on good terms with Israel. I will venture to say that this image planted the seeds for later movement toward peaceful relations between the PLO and Israel.

Indeed, such peaceful relations, though widely decried as heretical, were not so unthinkable as the anti-Sadat rhetoric portrayed. In 1982, during the Arab summit in Fez, the Arab League adopted a peace plan submitted by Saudi Arabia, which offered Israel recognition in exchange for full unilateral withdrawal from all occupied lands and recognized the PLO as the sole representative of the Palestinian people, a plan that Dr. Ibrahim points out "was remarkably similar in spirit and content to the Camp David Accords." That plan was revived at the 2002 Arab League as an offer of lasting peace with Israel in exchange for the return of Palestinian lands. In 1994, after the announcement of the Oslo Declaration of Principles, Jordan concluded an official treaty with Israel. Given its large Palestinian constituency (Jordan granted extended citizenship to all Palestinians after the 1948 war), the late King Hussein had to proceed with caution with respect to peace with Israel. In 1994, Tunisia and Morocco opened consular relations, though they were severed after the start of the second intifada, or uprising, in 2000; and several small Gulf states, including Qatar and Bahrain, have made trade agreements. Today, just about every Arab government, including the PLO, espouses the land-for-peace formula that they once found so repugnant. A few years ago and much to my amazement, I heard the Palestinian scholar and activist Hanan Ashrawi, speaking on behalf of the Palestinian National Authority, tell an American television talk show host that it was time for the Israelis to adhere to the full and legitimate implementation of the Camp David Peace Accords.

Anwar's prediction that the "Arabs would come back to Egypt" has happened. The Iran-Iraq War, which began in 1980 and dragged on through 1988, cemented Egypt's return to the Arab fold: other Arab countries recognized the value of Egypt and solidarity with Iraq. As a result, the Arab summit in Amman resolved to permit individual Arab states the right to restore diplomatic relations with Egypt. Two years later, Egypt rejoined the Arab League, and the league returned to its headquarters in Cairo, a significant decision for the Arab world—and a totally satisfying one for me.

In a speech following the return of the Arab League to Cairo, Egyptian President Hosni Mubarak renewed Egypt's commitment to the peaceful solution of the Arab-Israeli conflict. What is more, he invited other Arab countries to join with us. At the conclusion of this speech, Mubarak received a standing ovation, which clearly signified acceptance of Egypt's peace policy.

The 1991 Gulf War, in which the threat came not from the Zionist enemy in Israel but from one Arab nation to another, was a painful demonstration of the very lack of Arab unity that Sadat had been demonized for acknowledging so many years earlier. Iraq's invasion of Kuwait was a traumatic moment in the history of the Arab world. That the Palestinians sided with Iraq only deepened the crisis. The Gulf countries had openly supported, both emotionally and financially, the Palestinian cause. Why did the Palestinians turn on Kuwait when the Arab media were issuing loud and nearly unanimous calls for peace? In Egypt, we heard stories of the torture of Kuwaitis and the destruction of their property by Iraqis. The whole fragile concept of Arab identity was teetering on the verge of collapse. Many Arab intellectuals posed numerous questions and concerns relative to the nature of Arab alliance, many of which involved Sadat.

In the aftermath of the Gulf War, there were renewed efforts for peace. In 1991, Arabs were enthusiastic about the Madrid Peace

Conference. Sponsored by the United States and Russia, it brought together Israel and the Arab states for the first time. In truth, the Madrid conference, albeit delayed exactly fourteen years, was a response similar to Sadat's invitation to the parties to meet in Cairo. According to Dr. Ibrahim, even the agenda and terms of reference were the same. Nevertheless, the official discussions in Madrid in 1991 marked a reinvigoration of the peace process. This new energy was carried over into the Oslo talks, secret meetings between Israel and the PLO that began in 1993 and culminated in the Oslo Accords, which called for mutual recognition between Israel and the PLO, phased withdrawal of Israel from much of the occupied territories, and the creation of the Palestinian National Authority to govern them.

In 1994, Arafat was allowed to return from exile in Tunis to Gaza. These new efforts on behalf of peace brought to an end the first Palestinian intifada, which had begun in 1987 as a low-tech, grassroots revolt, waged by stone-throwing youths. Over the next five years, general strikes, boycotts, and acts of civil disobedience and violence occasioned terrible reprisals from the Israeli defense forces. As a result of the intifada, the situation of the Palestinians living in Israel and the occupied territories was dramatically changed. Prior to the uprising, they had enjoyed comparative freedom of movement; afterward, however, Israeli security measures imposed severe restrictions. Curfews, barriers, and checkpoints became part of everyday life. Not surprisingly, the fury and misery this caused also helped fundamentalists increase their own hold on the population.

Hamas was formed after the outbreak of the first intifada. Dedicated to Palestinian nationalism and fundamentalist Islam, fiercely opposed to the Oslo talks and subsequent accords, its charter calls for the destruction of Israel and the creation of an Islamic state in

Palestine. Since 1993, its military wing has authorized suicide bombings as a means of striking out at the Israeli occupiers. However, it is also true that armed struggle is only part of Hamas's mission. Since its inception, the organization has been furnishing Palestinians with badly needed social services, including schools, mosques, and clinics. Indeed, it is this outreach, as well as its reputation for honesty, that has won Hamas a place in the hearts and, in 2006, the democratically elected government, of Palestinians. This has added a significant complication to the peace process, since, at the time of this writing, neither Israel nor the United States is prepared to recognize Hamas, a group on America's official list of terrorist organizations.

In any case, in 1993, the renewed peace process was welcome indeed. I remember the events with particular clarity, because the announcement of the agreement between the PLO and the Israeli government brought me telephone calls at all hours, day and night. I was more than delighted to comment. Journalists from Egypt, Israel, Germany, France, Canada, and the United States wanted to know what I was thinking and, more important, what I was feeling about all that was happening between Israel and the PLO. When news of the agreement broke, I was with my family in Egypt, so I did not know that President Clinton had invited me to the signing ceremony on September 13. I had somehow overlooked the envelope from the White House when I went through the mounds of mail waiting for me on my return to Virginia.

Early on the day of the ceremony, a limousine arrived to take me to the White House for interviews on the South Lawn. I was shuttled from one platform to another to talk with correspondents from all of the major American networks—ABC, NBC, CBS, and CNN—as well as German, Israeli, and Egyptian television stations.

The day—one that I had waited years to witness—was beautiful, bright, and sunny. I had been praying for so long for the day that the PLO and the Israelis would take the first crucial step toward peace—their recognition of each other's existence.

President Carter, who had also been waiting for this day, and I sat together for several interviews. We were both beaming as we expressed the same deep satisfaction of knowing that what my husband had started was finally opening a new chapter of peace in the Middle East. I had to pinch myself a few times to make sure it was really happening. In my heart, I believe President Carter and I were both silently thinking of another time, long ago, on that same lawn on a bright, crisp March day in 1979. Indeed, it was hard not to: Clinton, Rabin, and Arafat were sitting behind the exact table Carter, Begin, and Sadat had used the day they signed the Camp David Peace Accords. The same drama was being acted out for millions of television viewers, just as they had been almost fifteen years before. True, the actors were the understudies of the stars I remember, and the new script was radically altered, but the sense of promise was the same. There was great enthusiasm shown for the Gaza-Jericho phase of the Declaration of Principles, hammered out at Oslo not only by the Arabs, but also by the European countries, the United States, and even Japan.

As I watched Rabin and Arafat exchange a somewhat reluctant handshake, I could not hold back tears. I knew Anwar's soul was very happy and satisfied looking down on us, and I allowed myself to bask in this shared joy, to give myself over to the pleasure of seeing my old friends, including President Carter, Henry Kissinger, and Leah Rabin. Early in the ceremony, she and I had caught each other's eye, waving enthusiastically and throwing each other kisses. I knew—both by looking at her and from experience—that she was floating on air. At the conclusion of the ceremony, President Clinton, Chairman Arafat, and Prime Minister Rabin left the dais to greet, shake hands with, and receive congratulations from the front row of dignitaries. When Rabin reached his wife, who was seated not too far from me, I could see her speaking to him before he turned in my direction. When he spotted me, he walked back to where I was seated, reached over several chairs and between several people to take my hand. Holding my hand in his, he said, "When I was signing, your husband's face was in front of me." Tears filled my eyes as I said, "Mine, too!"

Later, in October 1993, I received this letter. It is one of my most treasured possessions:

Dear Mrs. El-Sadat,

I was very moved to read the interview you gave Mrs. Smadar Perry [Middle East editor of Yediot Aharonot*], and I express my deepest affection and admiration for your outspoken and open support. I would like to stress that I hold the utmost respect for the late President Anwar El-Sadat whom I admired for his statesmanship, great courage and sacrifice for the sake of peace. I have made it my personal commitment to strive tirelessly and not to leave a stone unturned in my constant search for peace between Israel and its Arab neighbors. Your late husband's efforts for peace serve as a shining example for my firm determination toward reconciliation between Israelis and Arabs in this area of the world.*

Dear Mrs. Sadat, I follow your statements very closely and I have the highest praise for your comments and perseverance. I wish you the best of luck in your endeavors for the sake of peace.

Sincerely,
Yitzak Rabin

Two years later, Rabin was gone, struck down by an enemy of peace, another extremist obsessed with the distorted and absurd idea that anyone who brings peace to the Middle East must die.

When I heard the news of Rabin's assassination, I was in my home in Virginia. It was a crisp, sunny November day, and I was painting when one of my children called from Cairo. They had hoped that I had not heard the news on the television before one of them could tell me. I had not, and I was speechless at the news. For a moment, I had no sensation of breathing, of time and place. I was silent, but my heart called out, "Anwar!" All of my life, I have tried to put terrible memories aside. As a child, I tried immediately to forget things that had frightened or hurt me. I am a woman living for today and tomorrow, but on that day, I could not suppress my memories, my fears, my anger. Seeing the face of the man who had done this terrible thing was too much. All the painful memories of October 6, 1981, took over. First, Sadat, now Rabin.

I wanted to talk to Leah Rabin, but I was loath to disturb her at so difficult a time. Instead I contacted the Israeli ambassador to ask if he would convey my letter of sympathy to Mrs. Rabin. I wanted her to know right away that she was in my prayers. A few days later, I called Israel to speak to Leah myself. This is what I said:

Leah, I know you are a strong woman, but I want you to be even stronger now. I know what you are going through. I know your heart is broken. You are suffering. Your children are suffering. But I want you to act with the same courage as your husband. I want you to stand proudly and carry your husband's message of peace. This is what I am doing. Yes, our husbands have been taken from us. We cannot change that, but we must never, ever give up. We have to go on, for our children and for our husbands. They would want us to do this. Leah, God will help us.

Leah and I saw each other several times after the death of her husband, and she and I were together for the Norman and Florence Brody Family Public Policy Forum, Two Women of Peace: A Conversation with Leah Rabin and Jehan Sadat, for the University of Maryland. She and I are renowned for our candor, so having both of us together made for a lively, honest dialogue. After that, she and I, along with Farah Diba Pahlavi, the Shahbanu of Iran, were scheduled to attend a dinner sponsored by the Friends of Tel Aviv University. The three of us were being honored for being Women of Peace in the Middle East. Leah, however, was too ill from cancer to attend. Months later, I saw her last television interview, delivered from her deathbed. She was visibly weak in body, but her voice for peace was strong. Immaculately dressed and wearing makeup, with her hair finely coiffed, she strongly urged the Israeli leadership to end the violence in the Middle East. Watching her, I was again full of admiration, and sadness.

In 1996, Leah had campaigned on behalf of Shimon Peres, who, along with Rabin and Arafat, shared the 1994 Nobel Peace Prize for their work on the Oslo agreements. In the wake of Rabin's death, Peres had served as prime minister for six months and had pledged to continue the peace initiative. Despite Leah's help, Peres lost. Instead, a string of Hamas suicide bombings in spring 1996 helped propel Likud leader Benjamin Netanyahu into office. Although personally opposed to the Oslo agreements, he nevertheless promised to continue with the implementation of the process to which his country had committed. Time proved that he never sincerely wanted to make peace with Arafat and the

Palestinians. Indeed, his three-year administration was marked by actions that undermined the accords: in particular, his decision in 1996 to open a controversial gate between two tunnels in the old City of Jerusalem, which Palestinians believed would endanger the foundations of the nearby Al-Aqsa Mosque, caused days of rioting and dozens of deaths.

When he was voted out, I transferred my hopes to Ehud Barak, who not only had a mandate from his people to make peace, but also expressed his support for Sadat's bold methods. At last, I thought, we have someone with the will to bring peace. I hoped that with the support of the United States—President Clinton was personally involved in the negotiations—peace in the Middle East might well be within reach. In July 2000, Clinton convened a summit at Camp David with Barak and Arafat. I can still see Barak and Arafat hesitating as they tried to decide who would go in the double door to the meeting room first. On the surface, it was a humorous image, but it also foreshadowed their inability to cross a new threshold.

I, like so much of the rest of the world, was crushed when the 2000 Camp David talks collapsed. I am not certain there is any utility in establishing who was to blame for the failure, or if any single party bears responsibility. Clinton clearly held Arafat responsible, but reports from various members of the negotiating teams and the journalists who followed the negotiations conflict. What is certain is that Arafat and Barak's inability to come to terms unleashed another bloody cycle of violence. The second, or Al-Aqsa, intifada was triggered by Ariel Sharon's highly public September visit to the compound containing the Aqsa Mosque, surrounded by a Likud party delegation and hundreds of Israeli riot police. The stated purpose was to assert the right of all Israelis to visit the Temple Mount, which is part of the same compound, but it was widely viewed by

Palestinians as a deliberate provocation. The next day, September 29, 2000, a stone-throwing demonstration by a Palestinian crowd ended with Israeli police opening fire and killing four of the protesters. So when, in late December 2000, in the final weeks of Clinton's second term, a deadline for the Palestinians and Israelis was set, I was not optimistic. Not only did I doubt that the parties could do what they claimed they would, I feared that the violence would intensify when they failed. There is little satisfaction in noting that I was right. Clinton's push would also mark an end to an era in America's leadership role in mediating the Arab-Israeli conflict.

Indeed, as I look back over the years since the first Camp David talks, there have been two stages. The first was a maddening sort of dance—one step forward, two steps back, two steps forward, then one step back—in which it seemed Israel and the Arabs were moving toward solutions and peace. Then suddenly the dance ended, and the dirge of death and destruction began. The massacre at the Ibrahimi Mosque in Hebron in 1994, the opening of the tunnel near Al-Aqsa Mosque in 1996, the presence of more than 150 Jewish settlements in the territories, the construction of more than 6,500 Jewish housing units in the Har Homa settlement on Jabal Abu Ghnein in 1997, the creation of more than 16,000 additional housing units in Jerusalem with plans for the construction of more in East Jerusalem and the West Bank, and the confiscation of more and more Arab land, the demolition of Arab homes, the expansion of Jerusalem's boundaries, the war on terrorism, the incursion into Palestinian territory, the stand-off at the Church of the Nativity in 2002, the siege at Arafat's compound, Jenin, Nablus, Qalqilya, Telkarum, the university bombing, the curfews, the tanks, the F16s, the bulldozers, the suicide bombers, the mangled buses and cars: these attacks and counterattacks stopped all negotiations. The list of intrusions and infractions and injustices goes on and on. Where does America stand? The United Nations? Putting the peace train back on track will require more than warnings and political posturing. What would happen, I wonder, if all of the Palestinians and Israelis who want peace marched into the streets and said, "Enough"? The people, Arabs and Israelis, need peace. We want peace. We want an end to the strife, poverty, and iniquities between Palestinians and Israelis. The Palestinians deserve their state and their rights; the Israelis deserve to live in peace with their neighbors.

When Sharon was elected Israeli prime minister in 2000, I knew immediately that the Middle East was entering a troubled period. Arabs almost universally reviled Sharon as the Butcher of Shatila. Moreover, the antipathy, even hatred, between Arafat and Sharon was too deep for forgiveness, too raw for reconciliation. And indeed, beginning in 2001, Sharon laid siege to Arafat's compound in Ramallah, where Arafat would remain, under house arrest, until shortly before his death in 2004. Confined by the Israelis and dismissed by the Americans—in 2002, President George W. Bush called for new Palestinian leadership—Arafat had already lost much credibility in the geopolitical arena. He could not bring the more militant factions of Palestinians to heel, and many members of his Fatah party were perceived to be self-serving and corrupt.

Meanwhile, Sharon acted unilaterally to begin building a security wall designed to protect Israelis from suicide bomb attacks but also to destroy and divide Palestinian lands further. In 2005, also unilaterally, he withdrew the settlements from Gaza. It was a necessary step but less in the interest of peace than in preserving Israeli security. Parsing his motives may be beside the point, for at the time of this writing, Sharon lies completely incapacitated, and Ehud Olmert, his successor, has just ceded Israeli leadership in the wake of a corruption scandal.

Following elections in 2006, Hamas was elected to control the Palestinian government with Mahmoud Abbas as president. Thankfully, Abbas is committed to peace. Olmert calls him a good and honorable man, and the world's leaders, including Bush, have tried to bolster his position; however, Abbas's own constituency has been less enthusiastic. Indeed, Palestinians were split between Hamas and Fatah following an outright civil war in which ordinary Palestinians were again the victims. Abbas has since attempted to administer the Palestinian government from Ramallah, while Hamas took control of Gaza where, until now, they continue to call for the destruction of Israel and lob rockets over the border into southern Israel. In turn, Israel has punished all Gazans—sealing the borders, turning off the electricity and water—in hopes that the Gazans will turn away from Hamas. The Israeli policy of collective punishment is a woeful failure, and the 1.4 million Gazans who inhabit only 146 square miles are literally prisoners. Conditions in Gaza are squalid, hopeless, and desperate. Not only is Gaza a breeding ground for extremism, it is also a humanitarian crisis. South Africa's Bishop Desmond Tutu, the Nobel laureate who lived through decades of apartheid and spent several years bringing the torturers and their victims to a point of acceptance, shed tears and issued a heartfelt call for peace and reconciliation when he toured the area in 2008.

What a mess, a deadly concoction of promise and failure! Add to the mix the fact that at the time of this writing, spring 2008, the war on terrorism is raging, suicide bombers and insurgents are unleashing their violence on more and more innocent souls, and Israel is still allowing the occupation (ergo, the mass punishment) of the Palestinian people. In the past eight years, America has seemed to vacillate in its Middle East policy. As a result, instability in the Middle East has festered and raged. Throughout much of his two terms, President Bush was disengaged from the Arab-Israeli conflict; his Middle East policy was, of course, dominated by 9/11, the Global War on Terror, and the military action in Iraq and Afghanistan. Understandable as it might seem that these other foreign policy concerns might eclipse peace between Arabs and Israelis as a priority, I am convinced that the successes of all of these are linked. I am by no means the first to say so. In October 2007, an open letter to President Bush and Secretary of State Condoleezza Rice, signed by a number of prominent Middle East and security experts, including Zbigniew Brzezinski, former national security adviser to President Jimmy Carter; Lee H. Hamilton, former congressman and co-chair of the Iraq Study Group; and Brent Scowcroft, former national security adviser to Presidents Gerald Ford and George H. W. Bush, urged the president to make peace between Israel and Palestine a priority. On the eve of the Annapolis Conference in November 2007, the first major initiative of the Bush administration to broker Mideast peace, they wrote: "The Middle East remains mired in its worst crisis in years, and a positive outcome of the conference could play a critical role in stemming the rising tide of instability and violence. Because failure risks devastating consequences in the region and beyond, it is critically important that the conference succeed."

Although this letter was addressed to George Bush, it could just as appropriately have been directed to the forty-fourth president of the United States. Neglecting the peace process is dangerously shortsighted. Moreover, the war on terrorism, with its black-and-white assessments of who is and who is not a terrorist group, complicated (and still complicates) an already convoluted problem and has allowed a heavy hand to fall on all the Palestinian people. Again, collective punishment is not the answer. Punishment of families and friends of suicide bombers does not discourage or decrease terrorism. On the contrary, it incites more hatred and violence. It can only breed more terrorism, mistrust, and ultimately vengeance.

Think for a moment about the tactics the Israelis have used to stop the suicide bombers: curfews, tanks in the streets, barriers and concrete walls, bulldozers, checkpoints. Have they been successful? They cause harm to Israelis as well as Palestinians. Why not make peace with the Arabs and unite in the war against terrorism? The constant struggle between Palestinians and Israelis is tearing the Middle East asunder, spreading death and increasing grave social, economic, and political problems. These conditions will not dissolve into thin air when a treaty is signed or when hands are shaken or lands returned. Treaties cannot decree the end of poverty and iniquity. Treaties cannot mandate political liberalization, and treaties cannot erase the fact that men and women need jobs, children need to be educated and a chance to grow in safe, secure, and productive environments, and finally, all women must be ensured equal rights. On the other hand, treaties allow governments to disengage from war and conflict in order to start the process of development and social improvements.

Generally, there are three major issues that must be dealt with in order to reach any satisfactory agreement: the problem of the settlements, the Palestinian right of return, and the status of Jerusalem. However thorny and complex each of these issues may be, it is worth noting that the two-state solution that most parties now embrace is, in itself, something that was once regarded as unachievable. Golda Meir once famously commented that the Palestinian people "do not exist." Yet in 2007, Israeli foreign minister Tzipi Livni reiterated her country's position to journalist Roger Cohen in *The New York Times Magazine*. "Just as Israel was established for the Jewish people and gave refuge to them from European and Arab states, so a Palestinian state is the homeland of the Palestinian people, those who live in the territories and those who left in 1948 and are being kept as political cards in refugee camps." Although the shape of these two states must still be hammered out, this is a sea change. Likewise, most Palestinians—and more broadly Arabs—have faced the fact that Israel is a permanent state and they are willing to have a lasting comprehensive peace in return for the end of occupation and the return of land based on the 1967 borders. Opinion has shifted mightily, and the accusation leveled by each side that the other will not compromise is historically inaccurate. Perhaps the greatest indicator to date is the fall 2008 interiew that outgoing prime minister Ehud Olmert gave to the Israeli newspaper *Yediot Aharonot*. The former right-winger said: "We face the need to decide but are not willing to tell ourselves, yes, this is what we have to do. We have to reach an agreement with the Palestinians, the meaning of which is that in practice we will withdraw from almost all of the territories, if not all of the territories. We will leave a percentage of these territories in our hands, but will have to give the Palestinians a similar percentage, because without that there will be no peace."

Settlements and Borders

These Jewish-only communities in strategic locations in the areas occupied during the 1967 war have long been a barrier to peace. At various points in its history, Israel has both encouraged settlement and, more rarely, forcibly removed settlers: Ariel Sharon, who exhorted Israelis to "grab every hilltop" and dismantled the settlements in Gaza in 2005, did both. According to international law, such settlements are illegal: Resolution 242 specifically emphasizes the "inadmissibility of territory gained by war," but there are powerful voices within Israel that insist that they are vital to its security, and others who claim that by right of history, the land is their own.

In *The Accidental Empire*, Gershom Gorenberg writes:

> The purpose of settlement since the day in July 67 when the first Israeli soldier climbed out of a jeep in the Syrian heights, had been to create facts that would determine the final status of the land, to sculpt the political reality before negotiations ever got underway. By the summer of 2005, just prior to the pullout from Gaza, the facts included 250,000 settlers living in 125 recognized West Bank settlements. Another 180,000 lived in the annexed areas of East Jerusalem—land regarded by Israel as part of the state but by other countries as under occupation. In the Golan Heights, which Israel annexed in 1981, 16,000 Israelis lived in 32 settlements. Until August of 2005, 9,000 Israeli settlers resided in the Gaza strip in 21 settlements.

The settlements, and the roads that connect them, which are off-limits to Arabs, have allowed Israelis to carve up Palestinian territories in such a way as to prevent a viable Palestinian state. The issue of borders has been further complicated by the construction of a highly controversial security wall, which cuts through still more Palestinian land, divides communities, and creates isolated enclaves of land between which movement is restricted. A UN report on the West Bank Barrier's effect on Palestinian communities says, "It is difficult to overstate the humanitarian impact of the Barrier. The route inside the West Bank severs communities, people's access to services, livelihoods and religious and cultural amenities. In addition, plans for the Barrier's exact route and crossing points through it are often not fully revealed until days before construction commences."

Moreover, a UN map of the West Bank, produced by the Office for the Coordination of Humanitarian Affairs, shows that Israeli civilian and military infrastructure has rendered "40 per cent of the territory off limits to Palestinians."

Despite the fact that even in Sadat and Begin's day, settlements were perceived as a barrier to peace—the Camp David talks nearly collapsed on account of them and a two-state solution—construction on them has not halted. The collapse of the Soviet Union has resulted in an influx of Soviet Jews to Israel; thus, these new communities are ostensibly constructed to house these new immigrants. There are, however, Israelis who believe that these settlements are a national liability, not only because they require such extraordinary efforts to maintain security, but also because they believe they undermine the founding ideology of Israel—as a nation that is a haven from oppression, and not an oppressor.

The question of settlements—whether they will be allowed to remain or be dismantled entirely, as they were in Sinai and in Gaza—has a great deal to do with where the borders of Israel will be placed, itself a highly charged issue. Some Palestinians want to see a return to the lines negotiated in 1949; others have compromised to allow pre-1967 borders, accompanied by some land swaps. Indeed, speaking of 1967, it is without a doubt that there can be no comprehensive peace in the Middle East without Israeli agreements with Syria and Lebanon. The issue between Syria and Israel is straightforward: For peace with Syria, the Israelis must return the Golan Heights, seized in the 1967 war. In 2000, the two countries seemed poised for a breakthrough. The same can happen again, but Syria cannot be excluded from the peace process. Like Egypt under Sadat, Syria wants an open-door policy, a new orientation toward the West, controlled pluralism, and compromise for peace.

Fortunately, since Ehud Barak's removal of Israeli troops from southern Lebanon, there are no fundamental territorial disputes between the parties on the Israeli-Lebanese track; however, there are armed clashes between Israel and Hezbollah, a Shiite political movement that grew to power in response to the 1982 Israeli invasion. In the summer of 2006, Israel launched an aerial bombardment against Lebanon in an effort to unseat Hezbollah. They did not achieve their objective, and many innocent people were caught in the crossfire. Again, the Israelis hoped that their offensive would prompt the Lebanese to turn against Hezbollah. Instead, in the face of devastating Israeli attacks, Hezbollah won support from the beleaguered civilians, who, regardless of sect, despaired to see the nation that they had so painstakingly rebuilt become the target of so much destruction. That this terrible war came after the tragic assassination of former Prime Minister Rafiq Hariri in 2005 and subsequent killings of Lebanese ministers with anti-Syrian leanings has made the situation of the country even more fragile. Nevertheless, it is worth noting that although political assassination is a spectacular and terrible tactic, it is not an effective one. The assassination of a leader, no matter how confusing or traumatic it may be, cannot derail the will of a determined populace. Sadat's murder did not frighten the Egyptian people away from peace with Israel, nor will Hariri's assassination or, more recently, Benazir Bhutto's, stand in the way of their nations' march toward greater freedom.

Right of Return

The second issue pertains to the future of the Palestinian refugees, generations of whom have lived their entire lives in refugee camps in Palestinian territory in Gaza and the West Bank, as well as in

Syria, Jordan, and Lebanon, sometimes within eyesight of the home and land they once called their own. For example, two-thirds of the people living in Jordan are Palestinians, thereby comprising the majority. The future of Palestinian refugees encompasses the greater issue of permanent Palestinian resettlement. No one knows how many Palestinians will choose to move to the future Palestinian state. No one knows how many Palestinian refugees would rather remain in adopted Arab states. Furthermore, no one can predict for sure if any Palestinians will ever be allowed to come back to Israel. The right of return is, for the most part, rejected by Israelis. The Israeli government fears the loss of their identity as the world's only Jewish state if the Palestinians return—and rightly so, since the Jews would cease to be a majority if the Palestinian refugees return to the land they once knew as their own. There are, however, compromise positions that envision a right of return to a Palestinian state but not necessarily within Israel proper. In addition, there is the issue of monetary compensation for property lost as a result of the Palestinian diaspora, but to attempt to view the refugee problem only through the cold lens of financial transaction is to miss the point. Indeed, it denies the Palestinians the very dignity and recognition they have been fighting for. This is a difficult issue politically and economically. The fact is that the wrongs done cannot be undone, and the sooner we realize this, the sooner we can move forward.

Jerusalem

By far, the most difficult and unsolved problem is the emotionally charged question of the status of Jerusalem. What happens to Jerusalem will affect not only the political, social, economic, and religious lives of Palestinians and Israelis, but also the hearts and souls of Muslims, Christians, and Jews throughout the world.

Determining who has what authority over what sectors will require global rather than parochial thinking. Sadat believed that Jerusalem should be an open, shared city where pilgrims of all faiths could freely and safely visit. Jerusalem should exist as a separate, apolitical state controlled equally by Christian, Jewish, and Muslim clerics.

The status of Jerusalem lies at the heart of any conceivable agreement between the Palestinians and Israel. Jerusalem is inextricably enmeshed with emotions, nostalgia, and faith. The Israelis, relying on history, claim Jerusalem as their eternal and undivided capital. In 1981, they annexed Arab East Jerusalem, and there are passionate and powerful voices in Israel that vow they will never give it back. Yet history also substantiates the Muslim presence in the Holy City. To Muslims, the City of Peace is our third holiest site after Mecca and Medina. When my husband spoke to the members of the Knesset, he said:

> I have come to Jerusalem, the city of peace, which will always remain as a living embodiment of coexistence among believers of the three religions. It is inadmissible that anyone should conceive the special status of the city of Jerusalem within the framework of annexation or expansion. It should be free and open for all believers. Above all, the city should not be severed from those who have made it their abode for centuries. Instead of reviving the precedent of the Crusades, we should revive the spirit of 'Umar ibn al-Khattab and Salah el-Din, namely the spirit of tolerance and respect for what is right. The holy shrines of Islam and Christianity are not only places of worship, but also a living testimony of our uninterrupted presence here. Politically, spiritually, and intellectually, here let us make no mistake about the importance and reverence we Muslims and Christians attach to Jerusalem.

For centuries, Jerusalem has been claimed by many and controlled by one conqueror after another wanting to impose his will on the defeated—the people who conformed rather than fled or were slaughtered. When 'Umar ibn al-Khattab, the second caliph of Islam and a descendant of the Prophet, captured the Holy City, he established the first mosque in Jerusalem and initiated a rule of justice and freedom of worship for her residents that lasted until the Seljuks, an army of Turkish nomads, seized the city and began a reign of religious persecution. Next came the First Crusade with its knights of Christendom to seize the city, butcher the residents, and defile Al-Aqsa Mosque and al-Haram al-Sharif, known as the Dome of the Rock to the English-speaking world.

Then came the great Muslim warrior Salah el-Din (Saladin in the West) to restore a sense of tolerance and justice to Jerusalem. Unlike the Crusaders, who had slaughtered the Muslims of Jerusalem, Salah el-Din restored Muslim and Jewish cohabitation to the city. Years later, the armies of King Richard I of England and the Third Crusade descended on Jerusalem to confront the soldiers of Salah el-Din. The two armies clashed fiercely, but neither side gained clear victory. After several attempts to defeat each other, Richard and Salah el-Din acknowledged their impasse and agreed to provisions that gave each side certain rights. History shows us that a fair and noble agreement can render Jerusalem safe and open to all believers. Agreements and compromises can be crafted in the most adverse of circumstances if the leaders wish it so.

Although it is beyond the scope of this book to explore the many worthy proposals that peace organizations, think tanks, and governments have devised to bridge the gap between parties and craft compromise positions, they do exist. One in particular is the Geneva Initiative. Born out of the Taba talks, which began when Oslo faltered, the Geneva Initiative is an unofficial peace plan put together by influential Palestinians and Israelis and released in 2003. According to its mission statement, it is "a joint Israeli–Palestinian effort that suggests a detailed model for a peace agreement to end the Israeli–Palestinian conflict—proving that peace is possible, demonstrating that partners for peace do exist and that there is a solution to every problem."

Lack of ideas is not the overwhelming hurdle, but rather the lack of political will and personal courage. Peace in the Middle East requires leaders to place their people before and above themselves, regardless of their own personal risks. Even setting timetables and preconditions that seem impossible in comparison to the complexities of the issues cannot impede peace if the sides decide to compromise for peace. The Camp David Peace Accords were reached in less than two weeks of intense, frustrating, and discouraging but ultimately productive negotiations. In speaking of the peace process in Northern Ireland, Senator George Mitchell, special envoy to Northern Ireland, said there were days of failure followed by one day, the last day, of success. The one day of success, he added, makes all the difference. Years of futility did not distract my husband from his quest for peace. It should not distract us now.

Sadat's Principles

As the widow of Anwar Sadat, I cannot count myself an objective analyst of his policies, but I am not the only one who believes that the world is poorer for his absence, nor am I the first to note that statesmen of Sadat's caliber are in short supply. Perhaps, then, it is not so surprising that more than twenty-five years after his death, Anwar Sadat still has leadership lessons to impart. Indeed, today we would be well served to apply the following ideas—ideas that, by my reckoning, represent his principles for peace.

Accept That People Want Peace

Sadat pursued peace because he knew it was what most Egyptians, exhausted by war and desperate to turn their energies toward less destructive pursuits, wanted. And he knew it was in his nation's, and the region's, best interests. He put peace before his own political position, personal popularity, physical safety, or relationship with his fellow heads of state.

Although the details of the Arab-Israeli conflict have changed, this fundamental truth—that people want peace—remains the same. Poll after poll confirms that the majority of Israelis and Palestinians alike support a peaceful two-state solution, though they believe that the other side is unwilling or unready to meet them. Gallup reports that among Israelis, the proportion who say that in principle they "strongly" or "moderately" support the peace process is 72 percent; among Palestinians, the total percentage of those who said in 2007 that they support the peace process is 67 percent.

That peace is in the interest of both sides is undeniable. The devastating violence, corrosive fear, and shameful waste of resources and human life all testify to the truth of the fact that war is a barrier to all aspirations and endeavors. This is not, however, always true for the politicians in whose hands we place our future. To the leaders of some Arab countries, solution of the Palestinian problem signals the downfall of their rule. The question of Palestine has become the convenient hanger on which they display their internal problems. The same holds true for some of the Israeli leadership.

At the time of the Cairo Conference and the 1979 Camp David summit, minds and hearts were preparing for peace. Although I have dwelled much on the angry minorities in Egypt and the Arab world who opposed Sadat's dialogue with Israel, it bears repeating that most Egyptians supported their president's initiative. There was a remarkable energy generated as we practiced—slowly at first—envisaging a future in which our shared border was not a suppurating wound, our Ministry of War was merely a Ministry of Defense, and our sons and daughters might inherit a world less hateful, less fearful, and more whole. Inside Israel, the Peace Now movement had taken root and was flourishing. Indeed, the effect of Sadat's visit to Jerusalem is hard to overstate. In his book *The Missing Peace,* about the 2000 Camp David meetings, veteran Middle East negotiator Dennis Ross describes Sadat's trip as "a transforming experience for Israelis. All of Israel, not only the center-left, saw peace as possible. The effect on Israelis of all stripes was electric." In the United States, the powerful Jewish lobby was willingly adjusting its position, becoming more understanding of the Egyptian point of view. Even the world media, which had heretofore portrayed finding a solution to the Arab–Israeli conflict on the order of likelihood of, say, discovering the fountain of youth or inventing a time machine, underwent a great shift. Inspired by what they witnessed between Sadat and Begin, they too were preparing popular opinion for the emergence of a solution to the complex problems of the Middle East.

Such optimism has vanished. In its place, we see overwhelming discouragement, cynicism, and apathy. But this situation is not irreversible. The same transformations can be wrought again if, from the ranks of the men and women whose decisions affect the lives of millions, someone would step forward and publicly pledge, "I am ready to do whatever it takes to achieve a just, honorable, and durable peace," and then follow through. Correspondingly, concerned citizens in Israel, the United States, and across the Arab world must demand nothing other than Herculean efforts toward peace by the governments that act in their name. Politicians are prodigal with platitudes but all too parsimonious with commitment.

Be Realistic and, Correspondingly, Be Real

Anwar Sadat was a realist. Unlike so many leaders who define themselves according to a playbook of political theory, my husband was never rigidly ideological. He was an Egyptian patriot, first and foremost. He described his earliest political feelings as, quite simply, "a hatred for aggressors, and a love and admiration for anyone trying to liberate his land." Although his youthful ideas were seasoned by time and the practice of statecraft, he retained this basic clarity of vision. Sadat would not subjugate his own perceptions to political dogma. He had supported Nasser and the socialist revolution in Egypt, but years later, he would not, for the sake of ideology, remain blind to the evidence of its failure as an economic model for Egypt. Although our country had maintained a strategic partnership with the Soviet Union, Anwar Sadat was far from a communist, and conversely, though he was a devout Muslim, he was not an Islamist. He believed in the possibilities of the pan–Arab movement, but he could see that the Arabs were divided, and he did not want Egypt to suffer for a fiction. He knew his Arab brothers would punish Egypt for breaking ranks, and he knew too that they would someday return. He rightly perceived that only peace with the enemy—the same people he had spent his adult life struggling against—could achieve his goals.

Nor did he let ideological considerations determine his perception of his one-time adversaries. There were many, including me, who believed that making peace with a Likud leader would be all but impossible; Likud was synonymous with security, settlement, and the religious dream of "Greater Israel." I did not believe that Begin had the political will and personal determination required for making peace with the Arabs. Anwar, however, assured me that Begin would be a workable partner. He was right.

In addition to being realistic, Anwar Sadat was genuine. He was not without strategy, but he dealt without artifice. His straightforward approach to negotiating perplexed and aroused suspicion in the international and diplomatic community. Henry Kissinger writes in *Years of Upheaval* that my husband "was willing to forgo posturing for attainable progress" and that "Sadat generally did not haggle; he started with his real position and rarely moved from it." But Sadat understood the value of compromise and kept his sights set on the big issues—the return of Egyptian land, the idea of a comprehensive peace—and so in Kissinger's words, he was willing "to cut through trivia to the essential, to make major, even breathtaking, tactical concessions in return for an irreversible psychological momentum."

Today, such breakthroughs are nowhere in evidence. Realism has been replaced with empty rhetoric on the part of political leaders, who claim they want peace but impose unrealistic preconditions for achieving it, or they continue to act in ways that threaten the viability of the two-state solution they endorse. And it has been eclipsed as well by the cynicism of the press and people who say that peace in the Middle East is an impossible dream. By making it so, we absolve our leaders of all responsibility for delivering something that is achievable with hard work, political will, and courage.

Realize That the Peace Process Is Not Self-Sustaining

Historian Kenneth Klein described Sadat as the "engine driving peace" and, moreover, a "man in a hurry," who would not allow efforts to derail peace. When it seemed the proposed 1977 Geneva convention was being crushed beneath the weight of a thousand niggling decisions—the shape of the table, the seating arrangements, the order of the agenda—Sadat decided to go to Jerusalem himself and negotiate directly with the Israelis. Perhaps he fully anticipated the enormous impact his trip would have, or perhaps it came as a surprise—but whatever the case, he did not allow the "psychological momentum" that Kissinger discussed to evaporate.

As we know, the periods of pause, of neglect, and of indifference to the Arab-Israeli peace process have been costly to both sides: we have seen the rollback on previously agreed-to compromises, a widespread loss of faith, and the creation of power vacuums quickly filled by increasingly militant players. When their confidence in the peace process is eroded, people on both sides turn to leaders who trade on their fear and disillusionment, who promise to restore their pride or demonstrate their strength but who can only ultimately drag their followers deeper into the abyss. Both Arabs and Israelis need to be kept, and remain, on track. My husband knew this, and when he and Begin reached times of seeming impasse, Sadat recognized the role the United States could play as an honest broker and mediator. Sadat's intuition that the world's sole superpower must be involved in bringing lasting peace to the Middle East is no less true today than it was in 1979. In fact, given the U.S. entanglements in the Middle East, the U.S. role as peacemaker is in desperate need of rehabilitation.

A U.S. Institute of Peace Study group convened to look at U.S. diplomacy in the Middle East since the 1991 Madrid Conference concludes that U.S. involvement is essential for a number of reasons, including the U.S. role in offsetting the asymmetry between Palestinians and Israelis at the negotiating table. Obvious as this seems, it is also essential that efforts toward peace involve all the parties, and not be unilateral. For Israelis to dictate the terms of the peace will result in no peace at all.

Forgive

Jimmy Carter said that Sadat was "more inclined to look toward the future than to dwell on the hate-filled and often bloody past." Paradoxically, perhaps this has something to do with being Egyptian: we are heirs to the oldest nation-state in history, and thus we build on a foundation that is some 7,000 years old. I think this gives us a unique perspective. Because we are secure in a national identity that is ancient, vibrant, and overwhelmingly peaceful, we are free to be more expansive and forward-looking than many other nations. That Sadat himself took a long view of history was something that he demonstrated again and again, and not only in his certitude that his fellow Arab leaders would one day return to Egypt. This view fueled his relentless efforts to make peace with Israel and kept him focused when he encountered stumbling blocks. He wrote, "Whenever the Israelis created problems during the peace negotiations," he would "calculate again how much war had cost Egypt and the Arab world since 1948," and keep working toward peace. Such perspective was also evident in his relationship with the United Kingdom. Sadat had spent his youth struggling to free Egypt from the British yoke; he had suffered years in a British prison as testament to his conviction. Yet his hatred of Britain as a colonial occupier did not prevent him from developing close ties with Britain, a fellow independent, sovereign nation, once he was president. Sadat forgave, and he did not hold grudges, for he realized that they are ultimately more confining to the grudge holder than his object, trapping him in outdated thinking, holding him hostage to a moment in time. Henry Kissinger wrote in *Years of Upheaval*, "Sadat seemed free of the obsession with detail by which mediocre leaders think they are mastering events, only to be engulfed by them."

I try to share this holistic, big-picture approach to history. Speaking as someone who has felt the barbed point of the revisionist pen, I know all too well that the cycle of vilifying and lionizing according to political fortunes has little foundation in reality. For example, after the 1952 revolution, when nationalist fervor was at its height, both Mohammed Ali Pasha and Khedive Ismail, the nineteenth-century Egyptian rulers who together brought Egypt out of the Middle Ages, were accused of being foreign mercenaries intent on oppressing the Egyptian people. Orabi Pasha, one of Egypt's first nationalist heroes, who led a revolt against the foreign-controlled government, was called a traitor for protesting the cruel treatment of British soldiers. To me, such tearing down seemed counterproductive. How can we learn from our history if we seek to obliterate it?

I shall always remember my first official visit to Cairo's Abdin Palace, the former seat of Egypt's royal family. While walking around, I noted trace marks on the walls where pictures had once hung. Curious, I questioned one of the palace guards. He told me that portraits of our former king and queen had once covered the wall: now that the monarchy had been deposed, they were in storage in the basement of the palace. Unbelievable! It seemed an ignominious fate for so significant a chapter in Egypt's history, and although the guards regarded me as if I had lost my mind, they acceded to my request that every picture be returned to its original spot.

Anwar agreed with my instructions; indeed, he instinctively knew that we could ill afford to banish any part of our nation's history to basement storage. For some people, Egypt's 1973 victory erased the defeat of 1967, and so they believed that since Arab pride had been restored, we would again begin preparing ourselves for the next bloody contest. Not so Sadat. Though he was victorious, he did not trade on that victory to escalate the Arab-Israeli conflict, something he easily could have done. Nor did he use his status as "the hero of the crossing" to secure his own political gain. His goal exceeded his own interests, indeed, his own lifetime: he wanted Egypt to gain something more lasting than a military victory. He wrote, "If we look back through history we see the horrors brought upon Egypt by war—the martyrs, the destruction, the delays in development. Egypt became a backward country because of the slogan 'war is supreme.' That is why I opted for peace. I thought that without it Egypt would revert to the old attitudes, and I thought that it was important to create an atmosphere that fostered development, so that Egypt could survive and become a partner in the twenty-first century before it was too late."

Today, the slogan "war is supreme" seems to be the motto of all too many nations and movements, with equally calamitous results. More bloodshed in the Middle East is precisely what its inhabitants do not need—from any quarter. If we adopt Sadat's long view, American military action in Iran as a follow-up to Iraq is ludicrous; Israeli military crackdown against Hamas in Gaza, and indeed all collective punishment of Palestinians, is counterproductive; militant terrorist attacks against Israel are misguided. Each escalation, no matter how seemingly "justified," is disastrous to all. All parties must agree to open a dialogue with the partners they would prefer to ignore. If they have a part in the bloodshed, they must be included in its cessation. Sadat knew this and accordingly tried to assemble all the relevant players in peace talks in Cairo.

Have Faith

To include faith as a principle for peace in the Middle East seems at best counterintuitive. How can religion, which seems the source of so much misery in the region, do anything other than prove a divisive, countervailing influence to efforts toward peace? For me, the answer is simple: God, whether according to the Muslim, Christian, or Jewish tradition, enjoins us to treat others as we would ourselves be treated, to be compassionate, to be forgiving, to love our fellow human beings. God does not need to lead us to confrontations or brutality in his name. These actions represent the formulations and frailties of humankind.

Political scientists and historians have commented on Sadat's peace initiative in terms of strategy—his grasp of realpolitik on one hand and political theater on the other—and although I do not always agree with their analyses, this is appropriate. But speaking as a wife who knew Anwar Sadat not only as a statesman, but also as a husband, I understood that his desire for peace with Israel stemmed from something more profound than pragmatism. Sadat believed peace was God's will; he believed in Islam's injunctions to create a just and tolerant society. Sadat believed that Arabs and Jews are brothers, sons of Abraham descended from Ishmael and Isaac, and that they should be reconciled. In his address to the Knesset, Sadat said, "Ladies and gentlemen, before I came to this place, with every beat of my heart and with every sentiment, I prayed to God Almighty. While performing prayers at the Al-Aqsa Mosque and while visiting the Holy Sepulcher I asked the Almighty to give me strength and confirm my belief that this visit may achieve the objective I look forward to for a happy present and happier future."

Begin, Carter, and Sadat were men of deep faith, and all three were able to call on their own traditions and their own relationships with God to sustain their grueling progress toward an agreement. Prayer helped them stay the course. What was true then holds true today: we are no less in need of God's assistance. Indeed, that the faithful should not only include peace in the Middle East in our prayers, but also be vocal about doing so can help undo wrong-headed assumptions that religious conviction (whether Jewish, Christian, or Muslim) and violence go hand in hand. Faith need not be a barrier to peace. In addition, it is worth noting that like the man who questioned the Prophet, in order to achieve peace in the Middle East, we must trust in God *and* tie up our camels. In other words, we must make an effort: at the very least, let our leaders know that policies that lead to more war are unacceptable, that peace is possible, and we expect them to make it.

Some years ago, I had the great pleasure to participate in an original choral and orchestral collaboration, an oratorio for peace in four movements with composer Libby Larsen. The result was a major production for the stage, *Coming Forth into Day,* which premiered in Minneapolis, Minnesota. As part of it, I wrote something that I regard as my philosophy for peace—something that is, in its essence, a kind of prayer. I share it now with you.

We are all human and fallible, all mortal and frightened and weak. That is the truth. We are all manipulated by myths and partial truths about one another. Within our souls, we must remember that people are people and that we have been created in God's likeness. We all share a common dream, a dream of universal harmony and peace. Let us keep our dream alive and strive together to fulfill it. Let us unify our actions in one direction and move the world, day by day, bit by bit, closer to our goal. I put it to you, dear sisters and brothers, that we can really contribute to peace and reconstruction and reconciliation. The tragic yet exciting times we live in require more than ever that we as women and men of Good Will should stand together as one. Peace, true peace, is not the result of the balance of terror or a tactical pause in the armaments race or a cynical disregard of human need and aspirations by a strong power. Peace is a desire to fulfill oneself, by giving purpose and creative meaning to our short lives. It is a recognition that we are born to die, that we are all truly brothers and sisters and parts of the design of an infinitely Compassionate Maker.

On Being a Muslim Woman

MUCH HAS BEEN WRITTEN ABOUT THE ROLE OF WOMEN in Islam, and although the level of discourse has grown more sophisticated, we are in no danger of being overwhelmed by the truth about Muslim women. Indeed, there is no single truth, for Muslim women contain multitudes. We dress differently, speak differently, and think differently according to the nations in which we live, the extent of our education, and our economic condition. Like women of every faith, we share the same goals for ourselves and for our families: happiness, health, peace, and prosperity. We want to matter in our societies.

In 2005, as part of its project on the Muslim world, Gallup conducted a poll of more than 8,000 Muslim women in eight predominantly Muslim countries: Egypt, Iran, Jordan, Lebanon, Morocco, Pakistan, Saudi Arabia, and Turkey. The report, "What Women Want: Listening to the Voices of Muslim Women," published as part of John Esposito and Dalia Mogahed's book *Who Speaks for Islam?*, explored a number of topics. The ones I found most relevant to my own experience in working for women's causes were as follows: first, a majority of Muslim women believe they should have the right to vote without influence, work outside the home, and serve in the highest levels of government; second, most women polled did not rank gender issues among their primary concerns, instead naming other issues—lack of unity among Muslim nations, violent extremism, and political and economic corruption—as more urgent. The pollsters also explicitly pointed out that the headscarf, veil, or hijab, or indeed, any variation on the theme of Islamic dress (burka, abeya, chador) was never mentioned by any of the respondents. Once again it emphasized for me that the West's perception of the experience of Muslim women is quite different from the way we actually live.

More than twenty years ago, I sat for an interview with the late Peter Jennings, who was based in Cairo during my husband's presidency. About ten minutes into our exchange, he fixed me with a look of grave intensity—one I had come to recognize as the look that signals a reporter is about to ask a Very Important Question. "Mrs. Sadat." Jennings paused. "How many times a day does the president beat you?" With a straight face, I replied, "Twenty-four times a day!" Jennings looked as if I had just dumped a bucket of cold water on his head, and for several seconds, we sat in silence. Finally, ever so slightly, I smiled. Moments later we were both laughing so hard that the cameraman had to stop rolling. Since then, I have often wished that this exchange, disruptive as it was to the formal interview, had been captured on film so that Americans might have seen that conventional wisdom, even back then, regarding Muslim women was in need of an overhaul. At that time, the problem was, quite possibly, lack of information. Much of the old Orientalist ideas about Muslim and Arab women still held sway. In the minds of many, we were exoticized, eroticized harem dwellers, characters out of *A Thousand and One Nights* modernized by *I Dream of Jeannie*. Moreover, Muslim women were infrequently in the public eye: I was the first wife of a Muslim leader to have my picture appear in newspapers. Moreover, wives of Muslim leaders rarely performed official duties, attended state functions, or traveled with, and certainly never without, their husbands. My activity and social activism marked a dramatic departure from the political and royal wives whom I succeeded and those who were my peers. Much as I believed in the importance of encouraging, by way of example, civic participation among my countrywomen, this was not always an easy role to play. With time, I learned, generally the hard way, to consider my words and actions carefully. That the American press in particular treated me with great warmth and interest was a mixed blessing. On one hand, I was able to use my media platform to challenge misconceptions about Egypt and the Arab world and bridge some of the cultural divides, while on the other, I was harshly criticized by conservative factions in my own country as being "too Western" and sometimes for daring to voice my opinion at all.

Today the situation is very different: wives of Muslim leaders are routinely engaged in the lives of their countries. Suzanne Mubarak, wife of Hosni Mubarak, pursues an ambitious agenda of literacy and women's empowerment in Egypt. Whereas Emirati women once faced great difficulty getting a university education, today, three of every five students in public higher education in the United Arab Emirates are female. Queen Rania of Jordan has appeared extensively in the Western media, including the popular *Oprah Winfrey Show*, discussing her myriad initiatives. Sheikha Mozah, wife of the sheikh of Qatar, is a leading philanthropist and the force behind the establishment of Qatar's Education City, a campus of five leading American universities located outside Doha. Asma Assad, first lady of Syria, is a U.K.-born former investment banker who works to bring education and development to her country. These women represent just the tip of the iceberg and are only one more indication of the degree to which things have changed since 1970. Nevertheless, the efforts of high-profile Muslim women, whether first ladies or otherwise, to project images at odds with the old stereotypes face overwhelming competition.

The U.S. invasion of Afghanistan focused the world's attention on the cruel practices of the Taliban, particularly their medieval attitudes toward women. Unfortunately, in the minds of many non-Muslims, the Taliban became synonymous with all of Islam. The burka-clad woman became a mute archetype for the Oppressed Muslim Woman, and thereafter, it was not too difficult to imagine that this entire benighted population was in need of rescuing—and not just from a corrupt and inhumane political regime that took hold as a result of the spectacular misery of recent Afghan history, but also from Islam itself. Western concern about the "plight of Muslim women," well meaning as it may be, has often played into stereotypical ideas that we are oppressed and intimidated, voiceless and victimized.

Examples are ubiquitous. They may be heavy-handed, like Christina Hoff Sommers's 2007 *Weekly Standard* article "The Subjection of Islamic Women." Sommers makes no apologies for sweeping generalizations about Muslim women and goes on to critique what she sees as the failure of Americans feminism not to confront the "condition of Muslim women," which is "the most pressing women's issue of our age":

The subjection of women in Muslim societies—especially in Arab nations and in Iran—is today very much in the public eye. Accounts of lashings, stonings, and honor killings are regularly in the news, and searing memoirs by Ayaan Hirsi Ali and Azar Nafisi have become major best-sellers. One might expect that by now American feminist groups would be organizing protests against such glaring injustices, joining forces with the valiant Muslim women who are working to change their societies. This is not happening.

Although I share Hoff's outrage at the incidents of violence against women, I do not agree with the analysis she lays out in her article: that Muslim women are universally oppressed, in crisis, and prisoners to their faith. She is, however, quite right about the fact that accounts of lashings, stonings, and honor killings dominate the news, to the complete exclusion of more common and less sensational tales of women for whom Islam does not mean brutality or subjugation. Similarly, albeit from a very different place on the ideological spectrum, *New York Times* columnist Maureen Dowd lets loose an equally sweeping generalization. In a 2001 piece, "Liberties: Cleopatra and Osama," she wrote, "It is hard to fathom how a part of the world that produced Cleopatra—who perfumed the sails of her boat so men would know she was coming and ruled with elegant authority, signing one tax decree 'Make it happen'— could two millenniums later produce societies where women are swaddled breeders under house arrest."

Dowd then dedicates her column to a legitimate targeting of the Taliban regime, but her conflation of ancient Egypt and twenty-first-century Afghanistan, not to mention the implication that Muslim women from this "part of the world" share the same appalling fate, is both ridiculous and deeply misleading. Indeed, many of the media depictions of Muslim women—whether in pieces aimed at improving cross-cultural understanding or fiery polemics that warn the West to remain vigilant against the Muslim threat—seem amazingly one-note. All reinforce the idea that Muslim women need res-cuing: rescue from the veil, rescue from forced marriage, rescue from barbarism, rescue from fanaticism. While many fine books have been published on women and Islam, and not all of them by escapees from fanatical or abusive Muslim men and societies (though this trope remains perennially popular), chances are good that the image of a heavily veiled woman will decorate their covers, even when such an image has little bearing on the subject. Media professionals know that few images are more evocative to Western audiences than a shrouded woman, and so her eyes (for usually this is all that are showing) adorn the covers of literary anthologies, political polemics, popular histories, personal accounts, and everything in between. It galls me that people interested in Muslim women are invariably less interested in our achievements (for example, that four of the most populous Muslim majority nations have had women as leaders) than our so-called status as victims.

While it is certainly true that many Muslim women wish to shake off the oppressive practices and ideologies that presuppose they are less worthy than men, Muslim women do not require, nor do they desire, liberation from Islam. Islam is a way of life entirely compatible with and sympathetic to satisfying the aspirations of most women. A noted Islamic scholar, Muhammad Abdul-Rauf, wrote in 1977, "Under Islam a woman, like a man, is a responsible free agent fully entitled to civil rights. When she becomes of age, her independence is fully recognized." People, not Islam, infringe on the rights of women. Muslim and non-Muslim alike have been too quick to use our faith as an excuse to perpetuate customs that radically depart from the Qur'an and the example set by the Prophet. Time, tradition, customary law, and the collusion of men unwilling to have their authority challenged have combined to undermine the status of women.

The great reformer and father of modern Turkey, Kamal Ataturk, said, "Nothing in our religion requires women to be inferior to men." In Islam, men and women are, by nature, held to be different and are given different roles to play, but neither is superior or more important than the other. In the Qur'an, God addresses women in the same manner as men, enjoining the same moral responsibilities and religious obligations upon them. Men and women are equal in human values, religious requirements, civil and criminal laws, and reward and punishment: "Those who surrender themselves to God and accept the true Faith; who are devout, sincere, patient, humble, charitable, and chaste; who fast and are ever mindful of God—on these, both men and women, God will bestow forgiveness and a rich reward" (Qur'an, 33:35).

In marked contrast to traditional Christian doctrine, Muslims do not hold Eve responsible for Adam's sin and the subsequent Fall. On the contrary, Eve is accountable only for her transgression, and Adam only for his. Because both possessed free will, both were equally to blame for their disobedience. Moreover, Muslims believe that when Adam and Eve repented, God, who is ever merciful, forgave them. Thus, they were not cast out of Paradise for the Fall, but rather placed on earth in accordance with God's will. Islam has never entertained the idea of woman as "cursed" or morally inferior to men. Indeed, in Islam, Eve was not created as an afterthought or appendage from Adam's rib; rather, men and women were created from a "single soul" to complement and give comfort to one another: "It is He Who created you from a single soul. From that being He created his spouse, so that he may find comfort in her" (Qur'an, 7:189). Moreover, we matter equally in the eyes of God. "I will deny no man or woman among you the reward of their labors. You are the offspring of one another" (Qur'an, 3:195).

Historically, Muslim women have been socially active women

and warrior women as far back as the time of the Prophet's wife, Khadija, a prominent businesswoman in her own right. Indeed, the examples of womanhood enshrined by Islam are not weak, oppressed, or timid. Khadija's story is well known to all Muslims, so in citing her as an example, I need not resort to extraordinary acts of feminist revisionism.

Khadija was well respected in her community of the Quraysh, not only for her business acumen and wealth but also for her spotless character. It was unusual for a woman to enjoy such a high status: pre-Islamic Arabia was a cruel place for women. Before Islam, female infanticide was common practice, men could take as many wives as they wished, and most women were little better than chattel. Twice widowed as a result of the wars that plagued Arabia, she was reluctant to remarry. She had learned of Mohammed's reputation as an honest and upright young man and asked that he act as her agent and lead her caravan on a trade mission to Syria. His expedition was twice as successful as she had anticipated. Eventually her regard for Mohammed deepened into love, and despite the fact that she was his employer and fifteen years his senior—Khadija was forty and Mohammed twenty-five—she proposed marriage. Their twenty-five-year union was a happy one. That Mohammed loved her deeply there is no question, for he never took any other wives during her lifetime and was devastated when she died. Indeed, he continued to speak so reverently of his late wife that Aisha, whom he married after Khadija's death, grew jealous. According to the Hadith, she told Mohammed that Khadija "was only an old woman with red eyes, and Allah has compensated you with a better and younger wife." He replied, "No, indeed; He has not compensated me with someone better than her. She believed in me when all others disbelieved; she held me truthful when others called me a liar; she sheltered me when others abandoned me; she comforted me when others shunned me; and Allah granted me children by her while depriving me of children by other women." Aisha regretted her outburst and promised never to speak ill of Khadija again. Indeed, it is by Aisha's own report that this Hadith was handed down.

Khadija enjoys the distinction of being, of all men and women, the first Muslim. It was she who consoled Mohammed when, after his encounter with the angel Gabriel, he returned to his home, trembling uncontrollably. In response to his plea, "Cover me!" she wrapped him in a cloak and held him in her arms until he had grown calmer. When he confided that he feared he had gone mad, she comforted him: "Never! By Allah, Allah will never disgrace you. You keep good relations with your kinfolk, help the poor and the destitute, serve your guests generously and assist the deserving calamity-afflicted ones." In this fateful moment, and for the whole of their marriage, Khadija stood by the Prophet Mohammed spiritually, emotionally, and, with her considerable wealth, financially. Her fortune was spent in support of the nascent Muslim community, and she weathered persecution at the hands of her fellow Meccans with steadfastness and courage. Their union—a partnership based on love and mutual respect between two extraordinary individuals—was the first Muslim marriage. It could not be further from the stereotype of tyrannical Muslim husbands and their silent, subservient wives.

Aisha, who was certainly outspoken, is another beloved example of a powerful Muslim woman. It is thanks to her that Muslims have a significant portion of the Hadith, Islam's second most sacred text after the Qur'an. She recounted and corrected the stories of the Prophet Mohammed's words and deeds, including those, like the account of her jealousy of Khadija, that portray her in a very human light. This role alone gives her a preeminent place in Islam.

In addition, she was a person of formidable intelligence, resolve, and spirit.

In the years after Khadija's death, the Prophet remarried a number of times. Most of these wives were war widows, many with children, for whom marriage to the Prophet Mohammed meant the protection of his household. The exception, however, was Aisha, the young daughter of his close friend Abu Bakr. Intelligent, lovely, playful, and self-assured, she enjoyed the protection of the Prophet's household when she was very young, but she and the Prophet Mohammed did not live together as man and wife until she was past puberty, and such early betrothals were not out of the ordinary in seventh-century Arabia. Aisha was in fact already betrothed to a non-Muslim when marriage to the Prophet Mohammed was suggested. Likewise, that the Prophet had many wives is no indication of moral laxity in Islam or disrespect for women. Polygamy was the norm then (and was practiced by many biblical patriarchs), and the Prophet Mohammed was deeply solicitous of his wives and helped with various domestic tasks in their households.

Aisha, for all her youth, was not timid or subservient, and certainly not silent. On the contrary, she did not hesitate to speak up: she questioned the Prophet carefully in order to better understand the revelations he received from God, and she could be sharp-tongued and critical, even of her husband. Aisha outlived the Prophet by fifty years—it was in her arms that he died—and in her lifetime, she was acclaimed as an expert in medicine, mathematics, poetry, and Islamic jurisprudence. She instructed both boys and girls in Qur'anic scholarship, and her advice was widely sought by all members of the Muslim community, men and women alike. Her eloquence and generosity of spirit were legendary. In addition, she was politically active, in peacetime and in war—first accompanying men to the battlefield, bringing them water, and attending the wounded, and, in 656, leading an army into battle.

What have these long-dead women to do with Muslim women today? A great deal. For Sunni Muslims in particular, Khadija and Aisha are not dimly recalled scriptural figures; they are revered as exemplars of Islam. Their strength and accomplishment make them twenty-first-century role models for Muslim women around the world. That Muslim women can find within our own tradition validation of our individual worth, intellectual abilities, spiritual development, and leadership potential has meant that Western-style feminism has held limited allure. Muslim women, by and large, are not interested in proving that men and women are the same, nor do we wish to denigrate a woman's role within the family. Motherhood and family are exalted in Islam, and so rejecting them makes little sense to us. In fact, it is difficult to overstate the revered place of motherhood in Islam—the adoration and respect that most Muslim mothers command from their children. A famous saying of the Prophet is, "Paradise is at the feet of mothers." Another well-known Hadith (one cited by both Sahih el-Bukhari and Imam Muslim, two of the six principal sources of Hadith), recounts the story of a man who asked the Prophet: "'Who among the people is the most worthy of my good company?' The Prophet said, 'Your mother.' The man said, 'Then who else?' The Prophet said, 'Your mother.' The man asked, 'Then who else?' Only then did the Prophet say, 'Your father.'"

This is not to say that the home is the only sphere in which Muslim women can or wish to function. Nor should a woman's desire to work outside the home be construed as a repudiation of her role within it. For example, I always had a burning desire to be someone in addition to, not rather than, Anwar Sadat's wife and the mother of his children, though I am immensely proud of being both. I do not consider my ambition as a contradiction but rather as an extension of who I am. Much as I treasured my marriage, I wanted my independence and separate identity; the same is true for many of my sisters. Although we belong to a faith with deeply egalitarian foundations, we unfortunately face many barriers to full civic and economic participation. We have a great distance to go before we realize the rights that God gave us and the Prophet recognized.

How can we reach this state? In the Islamic world as in the world in general, success, freedom, and equality have one common denominator: education. To all Muslims, male and female, the acquisition of education is a duty assigned to them by the teachings of the Prophet Mohammed and the Qur'an, which commands the faithful to think, reflect, and reason. Islam is not a faith of blind obedience—for men or women—but rather one of active intellectual engagement.

Opponents of women's progress persist in the groundless claim that Muslim women do not require an education in order to be wives and mothers. This is absurd. How can a woman fulfill the Qur'anic requirement for all Muslims to educate themselves if she cannot go to school? How can a mother teach her children to participate in society if she herself is illiterate and ignorant?

A 2007 World Bank report by Talajeh Livani on the Middle East and North Africa (MENA) offers a statistical snapshot of hurdles ahead and the progress made. In 1990, the bank reported that 65 percent of men and 39 percent of women in the region were literate. In 2004, the numbers were 82 percent of men and 62 percent of women. The appalling gender gap in this most basic of life skills reveals that women, particularly rural women in the least wealthy countries, face serious barriers to education, whether economic (their families cannot afford to send them to school), geographic (schools are far away), or social (their family does not place particular importance on the education of girls). There is, however, some good news:

> In every MENA country, there is a significant difference between the literacy rate of the female youth population (between 15–24 years of age) and the female adult population, (15 years and above). . . . In 2000, the ratio of girls to boys in primary and secondary education in the MENA region was 89%. This percentage had increased to 92% in 2002. There has also been an increase in the number of girls who complete their education. For example, the primary completion rate for girls was 85% in 2002 whereas the rate for boys was 89% in the same year. These rates suggest that there is not a significant difference between girls and boys in terms of finishing part of their education. Similarly, the literacy gap between young men and women has diminished over the years.

It has long been my dream for my people to realize that when girls and women are educated, even to the completion of the most elementary level, society improves for us all. Statistically, educated women have fewer and healthier babies, and they take better care of the ones they have. Educated mothers practice better habits of personal and family hygiene, which effectively reduces the spread of disease. Educated mothers are more confident and more willing to encourage their own children, especially their daughters, to attend school. Educated mothers can help their children with homework, thereby increasing their chances for success and their willingness to stay in school. Making the education of women a priority is an effort that will require the cooperation of the citizens, the government, and religious leaders. Obviously literacy is not only a Muslim issue. And clarifying Islam's true position with regard to women and education can greatly facilitate the aspirations of many poor women.

Marriage

A long history of deviation from the actual words of the Qur'an and the true teachings of the Prophet has obscured Islam's attitude toward women in marriage. In the West, far too many imagine Muslim marriage to be a sort of slavery, in which a timid young girl is forced by her family into a union with a lecherous, tyrannical man, who rules over her with absolute authority. This is far from the truth. According to Islam, the woman always has the right of final approval of the man she will wed. Indeed, Muslim marriage is a consensual contract, not merely a religious sacrament, agreed on by both the man and the woman; therefore, a Muslim woman has the same rights as a man when she enters into the marriage contract. Because a woman's consent determines the legality of marriage, she can negotiate the terms as long as her wishes comply with the laws and principles of Islam. Once the couple agrees, they sign the contract in the presence of witnesses. Afterward, the sheikh pronounces them married. Although this process seems similar to a Western secular prenuptial agreement, the Islamic marriage contract is not a coldly calculated business arrangement. Instead, it is a profoundly serious commitment accepted by both partners to keep their promises in fulfillment of God's will.

In Islam, a wife has every right to dispose of her own property in any manner she chooses. She does not have to ask for her husband's consent. Any property she brings to the marriage or acquires thereafter is hers alone, as are any earnings she makes from her work. Islam has enshrined this right for more than 1,428 years. To the rest of the world, this practice is comparatively new. In fact, in

England and in the United States, married women were not free to own anything in their own names until the mid-nineteenth century and passage of the Married Women's Property Act. Until then, women's status was defined by the status of their husbands. Under this doctrine of coverture, wives could not control their own property unless specific provisions were made before marriage, they could not file lawsuits or be sued separately, and they could not execute contracts. The husband could use, sell, or dispose of his wife's property without her permission. And this was in America! Today, of course, these laws have been overhauled, and women in the United States and United Kingdom enjoy the same legal rights and status as men. Simply stated, it flies in the face of fact to believe that Islam is synonymous with the subjugation of women, while the West means liberation.

It is true that Muslims believe that marriage is the only context in which men and women can be intimate; young men and women do not date in the same way they do in the West, and all social contact between young and unmarried people is chaperoned. I know that our courtship practices seem strict and formal by American standards. I cannot apologize for this more conservative approach. Indeed, from living in the United States, I think it is open to argument as to whether the way in which love is pursued and practiced here is more conducive to marital happiness.

Americans in particular often imagine that Muslims are envious of the permissive code of behavior that governs social and romantic interactions between men and women; however, this is not one of the aspects of the United States that Muslims admire. According to the Gallup Poll, a majority of Muslim women said that the thing they liked least about the West is a "culture of moral decay, promiscuity and pornography that they see as degrading to women." Of course, it is worth noting that what some of these women doubtless regard as this culture of moral decay are the images projected by American television and movies, which, thanks to cable and satellite TV, are broadcast into homes the world over. That the behaviors depicted are not accurate reflections of mainstream American experience or beliefs is a fact often lost in transmission. I have often thought that American soap operas exported to my country are no better at capturing the reality of the United States than sensational stories about honor killings and terrorist attacks are at reflecting the truth of the Muslim world.

There is a certain irony in noting that both "Islam" and "the West" seem to find each other's treatment of women objectionable. I suspect that both sides have valid complaints. After all, women the world over—whether they are Oriental or Occidental, inhabitants of the developing world or the industrialized—have yet to achieve the full measure of political, economic, or social equality that we deserve. The challenge of any global women's movements is to recognize the shared spirit of our efforts toward full participation in our societies while honoring the very real differences between those societies. For example, it is not hard to see why Muslims did not embrace Western feminism, which was—certainly at first—closely tied to a sexual revolution that made sexual relations outside marriage socially acceptable. Yet contrary to the notion that Islam is sexually repressive, Islam expressly says that within the context of marriage, the pleasures of physical intimacy are to be enjoyed by men and women alike. Nor does Islam forbid birth control.

In any event, Muslims do not perceive decorum and morality as anathema to romantic love. Abiding by such rules for lawful behavior does not mean that Muslim marriage cannot foster true love. Islam instructs us that marriage is to be regarded as a joy, a gift from God, and the love between husband and wife an earthly sign of his presence. Men and women must cherish and respect one another;

we are, after all, two parts of the same soul. Although the Muslim family is, as in all Abrahamic religions, patriarchal, men are not given license to abuse their status as heads of household. Husbands are instructed, "Live with their wives on a footing of kindness and equity. If you dislike them it may be that you dislike something in which Allah has placed a great deal of good" (Qur'an, 4:19).

Before my marriage to Anwar, my relatives and neighbors were busy selecting young men they thought more suitable for me. As far as I was concerned, none of their candidates would ever be my husband. At first, I was infatuated with Anwar Sadat. He was a hero of grand proportions; I was a young girl dreaming of being his wife—and this even before I had set eyes on him! When we did meet that fateful day at my cousin's house, it was love at first sight, even though I was just as quickly certain my parents would not approve. To them, Sadat was poor, he was divorced, he was political, and he was too old. I was devastated, though not especially surprised, by their resistance. I was an idealistic young girl in love who would never defy her parents. I loved and respected them so much that it did not occur to me even to dream about marrying without their approval. In the end, it was not my tearful pleadings but Anwar's strength of character and honest demeanor that changed their minds about him and our future together. Thus, I married the man of my choosing. He was the love of my life, my eternal partner. Though my parents did not play their traditional part in finding my husband, it is true that the burning desire to find the perfect match for one's child is part and parcel of any Egyptian parent, including me. I did not force any of my children to wed a particular person, but I did play a significant role in their choices.

I know that in the United States and much of Europe, love is regarded as the sole province of the individual, with family considerations playing little or no role at all in the selection of a spouse.

In Egypt, however, where the sanctity of the family—a word that means not just the nuclear unit, but also grandparents, aunts and uncles, and other relatives—is paramount; to regard so momentous a decision as the business of the couple alone is an insult to tradition *and* common sense. In the closely knit but voluminous structure of the Egyptian family, both Christian and Muslim, marriage affects not only the bride and groom, but also the whole of the family, all of whom are called on to support the couple morally, spiritually, and in some cases materially as they embark on their lives together.

In Egypt, the idea of going it alone has limited appeal: adult children, both male and female, rarely leave their family home prior to marriage. Thus, despite the economic opportunities that emigration offers, most Egyptians choose to settle near their parents, sometimes—if space permits—in the same house. Why should we wish to cut ourselves off from the source of so much love, wisdom, nurturance, and assistance? All Egyptians, regardless of social and economic difference, share a reverence for our parents, grandparents, and other elderly members of our families. We respect them in everything, even in seemingly insignificant matters. My husband loved to smoke his pipe, so much so that neither my imploring nor even a heart attack could persuade him to give it up. Nevertheless, he never smoked—not even after he became president—in front of his father. Deference to this degree may seem ridiculous to people who come from cultures in which youth is lionized and age is equated with decrepitude and decline, but in Egypt, we believe our elders are oases of experience and wise counsel. Indeed, the primacy and sanctity of Egyptian family life is the bedrock on which my country rests. I believe that the strong and numerous ties that bind us to each other are one of the reasons crime in Egypt is blessedly rare. Even in Cairo, a city of some

16 million people, the crime rate is far lower than in less crowded, far wealthier cities.

Divorce

Muslims are expected to deal with the difficulties found in marriage in order to preserve the family, but Islam is not blind to the fact that people make mistakes. Despite the fact that a couple may have tried for years to sustain their love, there are instances when they may ultimately have to accept the failure of their marriage: a failure that comes not as a result of any innate wickedness but rather out of their inability to live happily together.

Islam prescribes equitable rules for divorcing without enmity. Neither the man nor the woman may resort to hurtful, humiliating behavior. Before a husband and wife can end their marriage, an arbiter from each family must help them try to reconcile. If this fails, the couple may part in peace rather than stay together in a marriage devoid of love and respect. Islam does not, in the name of God, condemn two fallible human beings to remain together as husband and wife in a wretchedly unhappy existence. Instead, Islam offers both parties opportunity to live apart and the chance to start over. The reasoning behind the relatively new concept of no-fault divorces in the United States has been a quality of Islam for centuries.

In giving women rights in the matter of divorce, Islam, without equal, protects the honor of women. A Muslim woman has always had the right to divorce if she presents a legitimate reason to a judge. These reasons have been enumerated and clarified by Muslim jurists, and although they differ somewhat among different traditions, generally a woman can file for divorce if her husband has not had sexual relations with her for four months or longer, goes away without contacting her for four months or longer, becomes mentally incompetent or sexually impotent, spends the majority of his time outside the home for his own pleasure and entertainment, asks his wife to engage in abnormal sexual acts, or violates other specific conditions cited in their marriage contract. The fact that Islam protects the rights of women to divorce does not mean that the society in which she lives does the same. Many wives with legitimate cause cannot get a divorce because their husbands will do anything to prevent them from starting anew, whether on their own or with new husbands. In other instances, the cases drag through the courts. And a woman can be easily, too easily, divorced by her husband.

Because I championed female empowerment when I was first lady, a small minority insisted I was determined to eviscerate Egyptian family values, and in my own home (as Anwar often teased), I had become a terrible nag on the issue of women's rights. I knew that my husband's plans included reforms aimed at improving the lot of Egyptian women, but I also realized that circumstances dictated that they could not be his first priority when he became president. In 1977, however, I participated in a committee aiming to reform Egypt's family laws. Family laws, or personal status laws, are the section of law in Egypt (and many other Muslim countries) that govern marriage and divorce, including alimony and child custody, as well as inheritance and employment.

Egypt's personal laws were established in 1929, and, in contrast to the rest of the Egyptian legal system, which is based on French civil law, personal status laws are based on *fiqh*, or Islamic jurisprudence. It is again worth noting that the Muslim jurists who have for centuries interpreted Islamic law, or Sharia, have not always emulated the Prophet's enlightened attitudes about women's rights, and there are great variations in *fiqh* surrounding family law. The family law code that governed Egypt was deeply conservative and in desperate need of reform.

In 1979, amid furious debate, the reforms we proposed were adopted. By contemporary standards, the laws seem conservative, yet they were perceived as a dire threat by the zealots, who perhaps glimpsed in them an erosion of the customary practices—particularly a man's right to four wives—that kept the law in their hands. Protests broke out in the universities even though we came nowhere near banning polygamy. Instead, "Jehan's laws" called for familial mediation for couples who sought divorce, made it mandatory for a husband to inform his wife that he was divorcing her, and made it mandatory for a husband to inform his first wife if he planned to take a new one, so that in such cases, the first wife could exercise her right to seek divorce within twelve months. Further, the reforms recognized the right of a divorced mother to retain physical custody of her children until her sons were ten and her daughters twelve, and longer if the court so decreed; the right of a woman to collect financial support; and the right of the wife to remain in the family home. We consulted with political and religious leaders at every turn to be sure all of our proposed reforms were in accordance with Islamic law. And they were. Islam never forbade women to work or vote or stand for election. Islamic history records many, many achievements of women traders and lawyers.

After passage of the reforms in 1979, my husband made another unprecedented move toward establishing gender equity: he decreed that women would be guaranteed thirty uncontested seats in the People's Assembly. *Quota* has become something of a dirty word in contemporary American politics, but in 1979, Egypt was badly in need of a quota system. Unfortunately, in 1985, most of the reforms were repealed on a technicality, and the seats in parliament guaranteed by presidential decree were lost. I was bitterly disappointed when many women, despite having the most to lose, did nothing to stop or, at least, alter the repeal. Some went so far as to support it, because they felt the reforms promulgated inequality and that men and women should stand for elections on a level playing field. Of course, centuries of male dominance had rendered our playing field anything but level. In 1985, Egyptian men were not yet accustomed to women in government; they needed ten or fifteen more years to grow comfortable working side by side with women in this new capacity. Then the laws could have been repealed; 1985 was too soon.

Much as it pained me to see this reversal, I purposely did not involve myself in the fight over the repeal. I did not want to do anything that might set Egyptian women back, and I thought my participation might exacerbate the situation. I hoped the people would appreciate the work I had done and would understand my silence. Happily, some provisions of the reforms were maintained. For example, women in cases of divorce could still receive alimony and retain their home and custody of their children. In January 2000, divorce reforms were again introduced and passed by the Egyptian parliament amazingly quickly. Prior to this, men could divorce their wives by simply completing the necessary papers and filing them with the marriage registrar. Women who wanted divorce on legal grounds, meanwhile, could be entangled in a judicial juggernaut for years. The latest reforms assign authority to special family courts to grant no-fault divorces to women if they agree to waive alimony rights and return their dowries. This is in accordance with a canon in Islam called *khula*. In the days of the Prophet, *khula* developed when a woman sought the Prophet's advice concerning her marriage. She did not cite specific legal grounds for divorce, like desertion or adultery, but said she no longer wanted to be married to her husband. When the Prophet asked if her husband had given her property, she answered, "Yes, an orchard." The Prophet then instructed her to return the property and thereafter consider herself divorced.

These reforms based on an old practice drew both strong support and sharp criticism. Some argued that if implemented, they would lead to disintegration of the family, for wives could too easily abandon their homes and responsibilities. I was reminded of the ferocious attacks launched against the reforms of 1979, when we were accused of trying to destroy the family. In reality, however, the divorce rate decreased following the passage of "Jehan's laws." Others argued that the 2000 reforms were not nearly strong enough and favored wealthy women. There is some truth to this. It is not fair to expect a poor woman to surrender her dowry, which is usually the sum total of her wealth. Here I should note that, in Islam, a dowry, or *mahr,* is neither a bride-price paid by a groom to his bride's family to "buy" her nor, as was the custom in Europe, a payment made by the father of the bride to his future son-in-law. A *mahr* is a gift of money or property from the bridegroom to his bride, and except in cases of *khula,* it becomes and remains the woman's exclusive property, even if the couple divorces. Such a gift is obligatory in Islam, and its purpose is to ensure that a woman enters a marriage with something she may call her own.

According to the legal reforms for women that I supported in 1979, a divorced woman was allowed to keep the family home. This is fair. No woman should be forced into the street with her children. The new law, however, assigns the marital home to both the man and the woman. This is ridiculous. How can a man and woman be divorced yet share the same home? Chapter 65, "Divorce," verse 1 of the Qur'an, says: "Prophet and believers, if you divorce your wives, . . . you shall not expel them from their homes, nor shall they go away, unless they have committed a proven sinful act." Further, in verse 6, it says: "Lodge them in your own homes, according to your means. You shall not harass them so as to make life intolerable for them."

The 2000 reforms also provide legal recognition for divorce in marriages that are legal but not registered at the public notary office. This type of marriage is called *urfi*. Young Egyptians who cannot afford formal engagements and marriages may be forced by circumstance to turn to *urfi*, which, like *khula*, is a recognized practice in Islam. So why shouldn't couples in this kind of marriage enjoy their full rights? They should, but these ceremonies must always meet legal requirements and involve the couple's families. If the man and woman are wed in a secret ceremony with only their friends present, their union is not considered *urfi*. The couple has not been legally joined; they are merely living together—to the dismay and embarrassment of their families and, most important, in violation of the tenets of Islam. When properly conducted, however, *urfi* is completely acceptable.

Polygamy

If the subject of Islamic marriage and divorce raises questions, the subject of polygamy provokes curiosity and controversy in equal measure. Although polygamy is commonly used to describe the practice of plural marriage in Islam, it is actually a misnomer. The more precise term is *polygyny*, which means the practice of a husband's having more than one wife at the same time. I will use here *polygamy*, the more familiar term.

Some think the Prophet adopted or legalized polygamy when, in fact, polygamy was accepted practice long before the advent of Islam. Christian and Jewish men, including their prophets, usually had many wives. In seventh-century Arabia, polygamy was a prag-matic choice. Frequent wars had left many women widows, and their situation, along with that of their orphaned children, was dire. Permitting a man to have more than one marriage—and granting women and children the security that a husband could provide—emerged as the most humane and sensible approach to a persistent societal problem.

Polygamy, albeit a lawful practice, is by no means an obligation of Islam or a right to be abused. If a man does take more than one wife, Islam says that he may not have more than four at the same time. The real caveat, however, is that he must treat each one equally in every aspect of their married lives. No man, unless he is the Prophet, can possibly do this. How could he? A man will always feel more for one woman than another, even if he does not admit it. No matter how equitable the intent of the law, how humane and practical it was centuries ago, polygamy is painful. Thank God, in today's world, it is unnecessary for a man to have more than one wife, even if she is infertile. A childless couple can adopt or live happily together without children.

Inheritance

There is one final point on Islamic law and women that I wish to address, if only briefly: a woman's right of inheritance. Though less sensational than polygamous marriage or the veil, it has also been the cause of great misunderstanding about Islam. Non-Muslims point to the fact that according to Sharia, women stand to inherit only half of what a man may inherit, and although this seems unfair, it is not the whole story. Islamic rules of bequest are enor-mously complex, and many experts in Islamic jurisprudence have devoted a lifetime to their study. Obviously it is beyond the scope of this book to explore this subject fully, but what is most remarkable about Islamic laws of inheritance is not that they are fundamentally unequal, but that Islam gave women rights to inherit. Period. In the Penguin Classics translation of the Qur'an, it is written in the chapter "Women": "Men shall have a share in what their parents and kinsmen leave; and women shall have a share in what their parents and kinsmen leave: whether it be little or much, they shall be legally entitled to their share."

Before the advent of Islam, wealth and property were left only to male heirs. With Islam came the directive, "A male shall inherit twice as much as a female. If these be more than two girls, they shall have two-thirds of the inheritance, but if there be one only, she shall inherit the half. Parents shall inherit a sixth each, if the deceased have a child; but if he leave no child and his parents be his heirs, his mother shall have a third. If he has brothers, his mother shall have a sixth after payment of any legacy he may have bequeathed or any debt he may have owed." Such laws revolutionized the status of women. They were in fact radically progressive, and thus it is endlessly frustrating to hear Islam maligned as inherently sexist. It is also worth noting that the disparity between what men and women stand to inherit occurs because, according to Islam, husbands, brothers, and sons are obligated to provide for their mothers, wives, sisters, and daughters. Regardless of a woman's property, income, or possessions, in Islam, the obligation to support her lies squarely with the man. Of course, in response to today's economic pressures, young families routinely decide that both spouses should combine their resources. I think this approach to marriage is only fair. Why shouldn't a wife and husband help each other as partners do?

On My Own

Accumulated to our beliefs, after Anwar died, my son Gamal was responsible for taking care of me. I would not allow it, and not because I had inherited a great fortune from my husband. Anwar and I were never wealthy, and after his death, I was actually left with some debt. Nevertheless, I did not want Gamal or any of my other children to have to support me. After all, for years I had been urging Egyptian women, and women throughout the world, to be self-reliant, to take their lives into their own hands, to stand on their own two feet. While married to Anwar, I tried to practice what I was urging others to do by throwing myself into projects that reflected my commitment to helping women and families. I began a women's collective near Anwar's hometown of Mit Abul Kum. At the Talla Society, village women learned to operate sewing machines, sold the goods they crafted in Cairo, and for the first time in their lives earned their own money and achieved a degree of self-sufficiency. Talla evolved into a large, thriving cooperative that provides vocational training not only for women, but also for men and boys. Some years later, I began the Wafa 'wal Amal, which, as I explained earlier, began as a rehabilitation facility specifically for veterans but later broadened to treat all kinds of cases. Later still, as a result of state visits to Austria and Germany, I helped to establish three SOS Villages for orphaned children following the model that the Austrians had developed, in which small groups of children live in houses with foster parents.

Eager to pave the way for women's political participation, I stood for election and won a seat on the People's Council, Egypt's organ of local government, in the Munifiyya District. There, my fellow council members and I sought to improve the infrastructure and the standard of living in a largely agricultural area. On my fortieth birthday, I matriculated at Cairo University, where I eventually earned my bachelor's and then my master's degree in comparative literature. Egyptian television broadcast all three hours of my thesis defense live to a national audience (an excruciating experience) but one I hoped would show other Egyptian women, who, like me, might have deferred their dreams of education, that returning to school was possible. I also wanted it to be absolutely clear that I had *earned* my master's degree; it was not given to me because I was the president's wife. Once my master's was concluded, I enrolled in the doctoral program at Cairo University. All of this is by way of saying that I worked hard to carve out an identity for myself. Suddenly becoming a widow, being forced to face life on my own, tested me beyond anything I had ever imagined. I felt bereft and frightened. Anwar was dead, and so was a part of me.

Although I am inclined by nature to keep myself busy, immersing myself in my work was not an option. In response to the stress and far-fetched allegations made against my family after Anwar's assassination, my children begged me to leave most of my civic projects. They could not bear the thought of my being pressured and falsely accused. And I did not want them to suffer any more than they already had. They wanted to protect me, and I vowed to do the same for them, but giving up the work that I loved, the work that, along with my marriage, had defined me, was wrenching. I felt rudderless, useless, and consumed by grief. For a while, grief held sway. I knew, however, that as acutely as I missed Anwar, I could not live out my life as the widow of the slain president of Egypt. I had to figure out how to move from being a partner, half of a team, to a person on my own. I was praying that something might come along to help me answer the question "What next?" I did not expect, however, that it would be a job offer to teach in the United States.

In 1985, American University invited me to Washington, D.C., to moderate and coordinate a series of lectures with prominent American women. Soon after, the University of South Carolina at Columbia proposed that I begin teaching there. As much as I wanted to jump at these challenges, insecurity held me back. The implications of living and working, even if only temporarily, in the United States frightened me. I was afraid I would disappoint people—those who hired me and those who came to listen to me. I was no stranger to teaching in a university or public speaking, and I had traveled to the United States on more than one occasion and felt at home in America, yet I was assailed by self-doubt. When I finally accepted both offers, I think it was because I was too scared *not* to. I consoled myself with the thought that I would be away from my family for only a few months. I could not have imagined that more than twenty years later, much of my life and my work would be in the United States.

Back then, just the idea of living in a place without fences or guards was overwhelming. From the time of Egypt's revolution until the moment I boarded the plane to leave for Washington—

some thirty years—I had hardly been anywhere without a security detail hovering nearby, watching my every move. Being without them was liberating but strange. In the United States, the smallest, most inconsequential details of everyday life, like carrying house keys and a wallet—things I had never done before—became symbolic of my newfound independence. I realized how much I had relied on others when, shortly before I was slated to fly to the United States, it dawned on me that I had not arranged for a place to live, and I certainly could not afford to live in a hotel for several months. In that instance, Henry Kissinger came to my aid and arranged for me to stay in a friend's home while she was away. I was as embarrassed as I was grateful. I realized that here in America, I was completely free—whether I liked it or not—to take care of and be responsible for myself, a feeling that was both exhilarating and disquieting.

For the first several weeks after arriving, every waking minute I longed for the home I had left behind. I dreamed of walking in my garden and along the Nile. I wanted so badly to lay eyes on the river that has always been my anchor, a source of pleasure, and a reminder that my life is irrevocably tied to Egypt. Most of all, I missed my children; each of the thousands of miles that separated us registered as a palpable ache in my heart. Why had I moved so far away? In an effort to avoid being alone with my thoughts, I was only too happy to dive into my work. I was teaching at two universities that are nowhere near one another, something I had not considered carefully enough when I accepted both offers, and I was working on my doctoral dissertation as well. This too filled me with anxiety, for I worried that I had taken on too much too soon. Before going to sleep each night, I would tell myself that as soon as morning broke, I would pack and go home to Cairo. In the light of day, however, thoughts of Anwar kept me from doing so. He had always encouraged me to think for myself, express my ideas, and be independent. My husband never tried to hide me or discourage me as so many Arab men of his generation did—and unfortunately still do. I knew he was proud of me.

Memories of our time together helped sustain me. In particular, I thought of the first party, a reception for the diplomatic community in Cairo, that I attended at Abdin Palace as first lady. Anwar not only invited every foreign ambassador posted in Cairo, but also their wives, something unheard of at that time and a prelude to another revolutionary act: Egypt's president entered the event with his wife at his side. This probably sounds trivial to Americans and Europeans, but it was of great significance in the Arab world. It was a harbinger of the extraordinary changes yet to come during the tenure of President Anwar Sadat. The guests were speechless, stunned by what they were witnessing. With that simple solitary act, Anwar publicly declared that the president of Egypt, a new leader in the Arab world, embraced the philosophy and supported the practice of equality between men and women. I was floating on air. I was so proud of the statement my husband was making to the world, not just about us but also about our country. The ambassadors and their wives watched in disbelief and unconcealed joy. They understood that they were not only being a part of something unprecedented, but also an unthinkable act in our part of the world. In retrospect, I am convinced that the reception was the moment when Jehan Sadat became an attraction to the Western media and a lightning rod for criticism in ours. My husband took it in stride, however, and he knew that I would too. In his eyes, I was a strong person who could face down any of life's adversities, and so, as I tried to adjust to my new life in the United States, a new career, a new sense of self, I could not let him down.

The first challenge had been considerable. At the University of

South Carolina, I knew I would be teaching, *really* teaching, American students. But what was I to teach them? I had no idea. When I accepted the job, I thought, admittedly vaguely, that my students in America might be interested in knowing about my husband, my family, and our life together in Egypt. Soon, however, I realized this material would cover at best one or two sessions. Moreover, conversational vignettes about the life and times of Anwar and Jehan Sadat hardly seemed the stuff of a college education.

After much deliberation and some panic, I decided I would talk about Egypt's feminists; surely, their achievements and heroism would be educational, interesting, and informative for American students. Furthermore, I was hoping my subject matter would give me the encouragement to make it through the class. I also wanted to tell Americans something about modern Egypt, which, though more relevant, is never as popular a subject as ancient Egypt. The tombs and temples of the pharaohs are indeed fascinating, but to ignore the vibrant contemporary culture and view my country as an open-air museum is to do Egypt a disservice. People are products of their pasts; they are not their pasts. How can Americans understand the modern Egyptian woman when their knowledge is limited to Cleopatra, Nefertiti, and perhaps Hatshepsut? I say this not to belittle our ancient history—for the tradition of powerful women is well established in Egypt, and the achievements of our glorious queens are part of every Egyptian woman's birthright— but I do think that it is high time that our pantheon of celebrated heroines admitted some more contemporary figures.

As I researched and prepared—a laborious process that involved handwriting my notes in Arabic and translating them into English— the more I realized that my teaching offered an unprecedented opportunity to challenge stereotypical images of Egyptian women, and Arab women in general. I was determined to eradicate all the preconceived ideas, dispel every myth, and replace them with the truth. I was, of course, setting myself an impossible task. After those first lectures about the women of Egypt, I decided that in my own way, I would paint an accurate picture of Egyptian and Arab women—without recounting a seven-thousand-year historical disquisition that my students probably felt was taking place in real time. I am, however, still convinced that people interested in the status of women in the Arab, and more broadly the Muslim, world are well served to learn, at the minimum, the names, the accomplishments, and the legacies of the following women. Why? Because by looking at their struggle, it is possible to see the way the women's movement in Egypt and the Arab world both ran parallel to and diverged from the same suffrage movements in America and Europe. Outspoken, courageous, assertive, and patriotic: these women are an antidote to the daily dose of shrouded stereotypes served up by the contemporary media.

Huda Sha'arawi is known in my country as the mother of Egypt's feminist movement. Moreover, she is considered one of the Arab world's foremost feminist pioneers, the woman who literally brought the feminist agenda from behind the veil, out of seclusion, and into the public eye. During her day, the late 1800s and the early 1900s, most upper-class Egyptian women lived a carefully circumscribed life; ironically, only affluent families could afford to practice the complete seclusion of women that had become the fashion, and a mark of privilege, among the Ottoman elite. Huda, who was born in 1879 to a wealthy family, grew up in the harem, or women's quarters, an experience she described in her memoir, *Harem Years.* In 1908, she founded the first philanthropic society run by Egyptian women. In 1914, she founded the Intellectual

Association of Egyptian Women. In addition, she and her associates were deeply involved in the Egyptian nationalist movement: as it expanded and gained momentum, the social and political activities of these women progressed in step with our country's march for independence.

The year 1923 was a momentous one for Sha'arawi, for in it she founded the Egyptian Feminist Union (EFU), the most prominent and only forum for women's rights. It fought for our right to be heard, vote, and stand for election to parliament. Also in 1923, on her return to Egypt from an international women's suffrage conference in Rome, she and a fellow delegate, Ceza Nabarawi, descended onto a train platform with their faces uncovered. Other women followed their example, and within ten years, the harem system and attendant segregation of sexes were well on their way to obsolescence. As more and more educated women joined the EFU, they evolved into a formidable force for educating other women about their political and social rights. The EFU was the voice of the feminist agenda, an agenda that included, among other things, raising the legal age of marriage to eighteen for men and sixteen for women, extending women's custody rights over their children, placing some restrictions on polygamous marriage, and agitating for the right to vote. In a comparison of the feminist movement in the United States and the United Kingdom and Egyptian women's movements, historian Mary Ann Fay makes the following interesting observation in "International Feminism and the Women's Movement in Egypt, 1904–1923":

> The demands of British and American feminists were different in certain specifics from the EFU. For example, polygamy and repudiation were not issues for British and American feminists, while property rights and legal personhood were not

issues for Egyptian women. The EFU's rejection of the private, domestic sphere as representing women's only role, its insistence on women's right to work and education and its demand for suffrage in order to enact legal and constitutional reform to benefit women were goals that were shared by feminist/suffrage organizations in Great Britain and the United States.

It is also important to note that the EFU was not an exclusively female organization. Various male nationalists not only supported but also worked hard to propagate its message. Some even served on the board of directors. In 1938, Huda Sha'arawi, along with women of similar beliefs in Lebanon, Palestine, and Syria, organized the first conference of pan-Arab women in Cairo. Once again, it bears pointing out that these women were not pursuing a separatist agenda but one deeply involved in the mainstream of political current.

Ceza Nabarawi, a close friend and protégée of Huda Sha'arawi, was another feminist pioneer. Severely and unjustly criticized for her activities, she was even publicly accused of flouting the teachings of Islam. Her response is as timely and useful today as it was a century ago: "We, the Egyptian feminists, have great respect for our religion. In wanting to see it practiced in its true spirit, we are doing more for it than those who submit themselves blindly to the customs that have defamed it." Unshaken in her principles and commitment, she steadfastly followed the course she had set to bring freedom and equality to the women of Egypt. She was the editor in chief of the influential magazine *L'Egyptienne*, and in the 1940s, she founded the Youth Committee to recruit young women to the feminist cause and later joined the Movement of the Friends of Peace, an organization that opposed the imperial presence of Great Britain on Egyptian land.

As is probably clear by now, education is an issue dear to my heart. When it comes to securing the right of equal education for boys and girls, one woman stands above all others: Nabawiyah Musa. She believed the education of women is our essential right, and educated women are indispensable to the development of Egypt's workforce. When Nabawiyah's mother, a young widow, brought her children to Cairo, she acted solely for her son's benefit. Like many other women of her generation, she believed that Nabawiyah could learn all she needed to know at home, by her side. Nabawiyah, however, was an intelligent, ambitious girl who longed for knowledge that transcended the domestic sphere. She enlisted her brother's help in teaching her to read. Then she began a rigorous program of independent study that eventually led to her qualifying as a teacher.

During her first teaching position in Fayyum, she was dismayed to discover that she was being paid less than her male counterparts for precisely the same work. Appalled, she carried her complaint directly to the Egyptian Ministry of Education; there she was told that male teachers were given higher salaries because they held higher degrees, in this case, secondary diplomas. What went unsaid was that women could not obtain such a degree, since they were legally barred from attending secondary school. Undeterred by the impossibility of her situation, Nabawiyah set about preparing herself for the secondary examination, all through her sole efforts, just as she had done as a girl. In 1907, she became the first woman ever to take this exam. When she passed, she wrote: "When the results of the examination were announced, I was among those who passed. I think I was thirty-fourth out of two hundred who passed. This news was well received by the [Ministry of Education] employees and by my fellow students. That was in 1907 . . . Had I conquered France my name would not have reverberated more."

At this point, the Ministry of Education could no longer make excuses. Her achievement forced them to increase her salary to a level commensurate with that of her male colleagues. Thereafter, Nabawiyah Musa was promoted from teacher to headmistress of a primary school, and finally she became the first Egyptian woman to serve as inspector of girls' education in Egypt, a position previously reserved for British women. Later in her remarkable book, *The Woman and Work*, written in 1920, Nabawiyah Musa set forth the standards for all working women. Her refusal to accept unequal treatment in the workplace established the precedent for Egypt's policy today of equal pay for equal work. She, along with Huda Sha'arawi and Ceza Nabarawi, made up the Egyptian delegation to the 1923 International Women's Conference. That the conference was in Rome is quite fitting, for these three women are the great triumvirs of the Egyptian women's movement. They in turn inspired and were succeeded by younger women who took up the cause.

One such warrior in the fight for women's rights was Amina el-Said. Amina, like Huda, for whom she had worked as an assistant, grew up at a time when the education of girls was of little concern, especially to rural families. Amina's father, a physician, however, worried about what would happen to his daughters if they lacked a proper education. In a decision that would be considered progressive by today's standards, he moved his family to Cairo where his girls could attend the recently established Shubra Secondary School for girls, which opened in 1925. She went on to attend King Fuad I University (now Cairo University), which, under pressure from Egypt's feminist movement, had begun admitting women in 1929— only five years after this once-colonial institution had been reopened as a public university. After her graduation in 1935, El Said went on to become one of Egypt's most successful journalists and magazine editors, and the first woman to earn her living as a journalist. She founded Egypt's first magazine for women, *Hawaa*, in 1954, and was its editor, writing a weekly column until her death. She was the first female president of the publishing house Dar el Hilal.

Over a career that spanned more than sixty years, she faced her share of obstacles and criticisms: she was the target of ruthless, unrelenting ridicule and personal attacks. But Amina refused to retreat from her work or back down from her stance on issues. At first, she published her work under a man's name, hoping that the pseudonym would protect her from the prejudices against women prevalent among the so-called enlightened intellectuals of the day. When her ploy was revealed, she was assailed with greater personal and professional criticisms. Undaunted, she did not surrender her feminist principles or her career, because she believed that what she was doing was not just for her own good, but also for the welfare of other Egyptian women.

Amina el-Said remained true to herself and her ideals until the day she died at age eighty-five. On the threshold of death, in pain from the cancer that consumed her, she would not accept the aid of a wheelchair or walker. Instead she insisted she could make it on her own. On the last day of her life, she turned to her daughter to help her to the bathroom. Just before reaching the door, Amina fell to the floor and was gone.

The life of Amina el-Said was full of courage and reason. She was dedicated to the cause of freedom and full and equal rights for women. With her passing, Egypt lost a stellar proponent of human rights and freedom, and I lost a dear, dear friend.

Another pioneer in the movement for women's rights was Suheir Qalamawi, a prominent scholar of Arabic who was among Egypt's most recognized academicians, writers, and feminists. During my graduate work at Cairo University, I was privileged to have been able to work with her directly; indeed, this courageous and brilliant woman was my mentor. Among the first five women to be permitted to enroll at Cairo University in 1928, she graduated in 1931 and went on to earn her baccalaureate and master's degrees. In 1941, she was among the first women to earn doctorates, under the tutelage of one of Egypt's most venerated writers and thinkers, Taha Hussein, who had been instrumental in supporting the women's initial admission to university. As scholar Margot Badran points out in *Feminists, Islam and Nation,* it is worth noting that her field of study, Arabic literature, was not an easy one for women to pursue, since rigorous instruction in Arabic had for centuries been the preserve of men trained at Al-Azhar. A staunch proponent of women's rights, Dr. Suheir sought and won a seat in Parliament, a position from which she introduced and debated policy on behalf of women. She also organized numerous workshops designed to educate and encourage other women to participate in Egyptian politics. With her guidance, I learned far more than comparative literature.

Today, I fear that the women of Egypt are at risk for losing the legacy left us by Huda Sha'arawi, Ceza Nabarawi, Amina el-Said, Nabawiyah Musa, Suheir Qalamawi, and many, many other ordinary Egyptian women who were brave enough to speak and act for the good of their countrywomen. Thanks to their efforts, Egyptian women have made astonishing strides in the last hundred years: we have access to all levels of education—women are half the 1.6 million students in Egyptian universities. According to one United Nations report, female illiteracy fell from 84 percent in 1960 to 41 percent in 2005. We can vote: Abdel Nasser granted suffrage in 1956. We have a greater share in decision making than we had twenty years ago: Egypt has female ambassadors and ministers in the government; a woman heads the government broadcasting and television bureau. Indeed, we are represented in all professional fields, including, most recently, the judiciary.

The fight to allow women to serve on the bench was long and arduous. When the arguments reached their peak, one of our leading justices was questioned as to why women lawyers should not be permitted to join the judicial ranks. He answered that the reason is simple: women are emotional, and therefore lenient and unable to impose just sentences. As appalled as I was by his attitude, his words reflect what many believe to be a fact. Many opponents of the advancement of women, men and women, claim that allowing a woman to serve as a judge violates Islamic teachings. Fortunately, Ali Gomaa, the grand mufti of Al-Azhar University, the world's most prestigious center of Islamic scholarship, issued a statement that Islam does not deny women the right to be judges or, it is worth noting, heads of state. If having a woman sit on the judicial bench is against Islam, why were there female judges in other Arab countries such as Algeria, Jordan, Syria, and Bahrain, some of which are more conservative than Egypt? Moreover, how is it that we can trust women to instruct and discipline their sons—sons who may one day become judges—if we are too irrational and emotional to differentiate between right and wrong? The argument makes no sense. Fortunately, there were enough of those in power who agreed with me. Egypt now has female judges.

This and other gains were hard won, and it is incumbent on the women of Egypt to honor the sacrifices of our forebears and avail ourselves of the fruits of their labors. Now that the battle for legal equality has been won, we Egyptian women must set our sights on assuming a more active and visible role in the economy. This same shift away from legislating equality and toward encouraging female economic participation is taking place throughout the world. Indeed, I have always been struck by the fact that the issues that affect women in Egypt are remarkably similar to those that women face in all developing nations. I saw this when I helped to organize a conference of Arab women in 1974, and again a year later when I led the Egyptian delegation to the United Nations Women's Conference in Mexico City, and at every subsequent similar gathering that I have attended. Today, equality in policy and under the law has, for the most part, been achieved (though equality in practice is still elusive). International resolutions are taking the next step and calling for the participation of women in development and decision making. I note this progress with cautious encouragement, for it was as recently as 1993 that the Women's Conference in Vienna felt compelled to reiterate the declaration that women have basic human rights!

At the most recent United Nations conference for women, held in Beijing in 1995, men and women from more than 185 nations debated the inequities facing women, then formulated strategies for improving our living standards through education, employment, and health care. They also developed strategies to increase the level of political and economic participation of women in the twenty-first century. The progression of the debates and theme of the discussions in these kinds of conferences tacitly indicate a definitive transformation in thinking about women, at least within the context of international issues.

The Committee for the Convention on the Elimination of Discrimination Against Women (CEDAW), the international treaty often described as an international bill of rights for women, was headed by an Egyptian female ambassador, Mervat Tellawy, for a long time. It has urged the evaluation of domestic work of women and recommended that this work be assigned a monetary value and counted as part of the gross domestic product of each country. Even in industrialized countries such as the United States, the potential economic impact of such a move is staggering. In Egypt alone, it is estimated that the majority of the work performed by women is unpaid, and thus not counted in the GDP. It is simply taken for granted. CEDAW (which was introduced in 1979 and ratified in 1981 by Egypt, the first Arab state to do so) has also called on countries to provide data relative to the status of disabled women and then describe the measures that will be employed to ensure women's equal access to education, employment, and health and social services.

Counting the work of women in the home toward the GDP would go a great distance toward legitimizing the real labor of child rearing and maintaining a home. It should not, however, be interpreted to mean that the house is the only legitimate site of women's work. Here in Egypt, I hear men, and some women, too, proclaiming that women should be content to stay at home, removed from public life. Though I realize that some women are weary of and worn down by the fight for equality and feminist movements, Arab and Western, which have not ushered in a golden age, I find this archaic attitude alarming. We live in an era characterized by the rise of democracy, globalization of the world economy, and the increasing importance of scientific and technological advancements. If Egypt is to move away from an economy built around agriculture and government support toward a free market and a privatized society (and we must), we will need to marshal the intellect, skills, and talents of every member of our citizenry. Right now, millions of women and their children are falling deeper and deeper into the chasm that separates the haves and the have-nots. As a result, the middle class, men and women alike, is losing footing. A woman's income can lift a family out of poverty, create opportunities for her children, and give her a sense of independence and agency that may increase her participation in the civic life of her nation.

It was not so long ago that women were not permitted to enter the Egyptian labor market at all. When restrictions finally eased, women were hesitant to seek employment outside the home. Following our revolution in 1956, President Nasser guaranteed government employment to all university graduates, male and female. Suddenly the number of women enrolled in university increased sixfold. More university-educated women were filling positions in the public sector. This act was, of course, noble in intent, but it was not sustainable. Assured of a job yet underemployed and generally underpaid, many government workers, men and women, gradually lost their sense of initiative and found themselves unable to climb out of the government's cradle. Meanwhile, the size of Egypt's bureaucracy swelled, hampering the state's ability to respond to the people's needs.

Today the Egyptian government cannot afford to employ every one of its college graduates. Although the state is moving away from its paternalistic role, it still protects the rights and safety of working women. For example, if a woman is asked to work after 9:00 P.M., Egyptian law mandates that her employer provide her transportation home. Women also have the legal right to three months of paid maternity leave as well as nursing breaks during the workday. Employee child care centers, first required in businesses with one hundred or more employees, are now available in companies with fewer employees. Unfortunately, some private sector businesses are discovering ways to skirt the government-mandated protection of women. As a result, women avoid conflicts by taking lower-paying jobs or leaving the workplace altogether.

If women are to be active in Egypt's economy, this attrition rate must be halted. It is not only professional and vocational training that women require, nor is it enough that they know they have a right to enter the job market. Women need the wherewithal to exercise that right. Projects designed to improve the health, employment, and educational and economic status of women and girls have been initiated. Projects to inform women of their legal rights with the goal of enabling them to benefit as soon as possible from economic and social programs are in full operation. Now that these governmental programs are in place, women must take advantage of them. This is the hard part. But to retreat now spells disaster for a nation, a region, and ultimately the world.

It is undeniable that men, Muslim and non-Muslim, still control the majority of power and wealth in Egypt (indeed the entire world), a condition that leaves women to progress only as far as men permit. We must remember, however, that men are neither our masters nor our enemies. They are our partners. This is a truth that many men and women grasp and that others must be taught to accept. In my own life, I was fortunate to marry a man who regarded me as an equal. Anwar was a strong proponent of women's rights: in addition to the presidential decrees that reformed family law and brought more women into government, he implemented an ambitious effort to support family planning and population control. Whereas between 1970 and 1975, Egypt had a total fertility rate of 5.9, it is now 3.2, according to a United Nations Development Programme report. It is not yet at the replacement level of 2.1, albeit far closer. Although I am proud to say that I played a role in bringing this and other women's issues to the forefront, Anwar did not implement such sweeping changes simply to appease me! He knew as well as I that women must participate fully in the life of our country.

It is worth remembering that such progressive thinking was

hardly his birthright. Sadat grew up in rural Egypt, one of thirteen children born to a mother who, like most of the other women in her village, was illiterate. Unlettered though they were, these village women were strong and capable. Unlike their wealthier city-dwelling sisters, they were not expected to cover their faces or live in seclusion. Of necessity, they worked side by side with men, and everyone understood that their participation in the life of the village was vital to its survival. What Anwar carried with him from Mit Abul Kum to the presidential villa was not the idea that women need not read and men rule the roost, but rather the conviction that men and women are interdependent. I relate this to make the point that possessing traditional values is not the same as being hidebound by tradition.

It is in this light that my country must see that the demands of women are not "feminine demands" at odds with our cultural ideals, but rather demands for Egypt and all of its people. Men *and* women want the right to work in order to secure their own future and the futures of their children. Men *and* women are concerned about unemployment, salaries, pensions, health care, political rights, and freedom of expression—indeed, all aspects of a democratic society. Just as our aspirations are shared, our success and failure are inextricably linked. Therefore, it is with great trepidation that I observe the current trend toward establishing certain women-only organizations. In the past, Egyptian women did not isolate themselves by forming exclusive cliques that promoted specific, parochial causes. They plunged into the rivers of nationalism that swept through the whole of Egypt. Egyptian women today seem to be trying to isolate themselves, wrapping themselves inside a feminine cocoon in order to live out their lives with the least amount of conflict. Professional groups and associations for female artists, writers, filmmakers, university graduates, and entrepreneurs are blossoming in Egypt, as they have elsewhere in the world. I do not agree with the gender exclusivity of such organizations. Although they are enhancing women's contributions in some fields, they are creating more problems. To achieve equitable and lasting progress for women in a conservative nation like Egypt, men and women must work together in mutually supportive roles. I know this firsthand; the reform of Egypt's family law would never have passed without the support of men, especially those serving in our People's Assembly.

In this book, I have spoken often of my husband's legacy. As for me, I hope I will be remembered as a feminist, an Arab, and a Muslim woman dedicated to the struggle for women's rights. I do not want to be remembered as a radical, because I am not. True, I have always expressed my opinions, but I have never been extreme in my views—except when it comes to passivity. I hate watching and waiting as if an injustice can correct itself or an ill of society can discover its own cure. Conventional wisdom in Egypt seems to espouse the notion that a woman's kingdom (forgive the irony of that phrase) is the home—a flattering slogan, I concede, but one that threatens to induce women into a hypnotic state of unrealized potential and possibility. It is true that a woman's kingdom is her home; however, she should not be held prisoner in her own kingdom. Make no mistake, I strongly applaud and promote the role of women as mothers, but I will never concede that maternal roles are the sole domain of their capabilities. Despite the rights women have gained thus far, a passive woman is prone to becoming meek and servile, dominated to the extent that she unconsciously relinquishes her dignity, her independence, her confidence, her property, and everything else she considers important to her, which ultimately has grave reverberations in her own society. Unlike the pharaohs of ancient Egypt who were buried with their treasures and symbols of their life's achievements, we mothers do not take our successes and failures to our graves. Our children are our greatest legacy. What kind of future shall we bequeath to them?

Egyptian women are standing on a plateau, trying to decide whether to move forward, step backward, or simply remain quietly and complacently in place. Why have women in Egypt, and indeed, in many other parts of the world, arrived at this standstill? I suspect because younger women have never known a world in which women were barred from civic and economic participation. Younger women take for granted the great gains made by feminist pioneers, and armed with choices and rights that their mothers never had, they feel less compelled to exercise them. In addition, I know that these gains have come with a price. Women—in Egypt and in the United States—have not yet arrived at a point where those who wish to raise families and have successful careers can comfortably "have it all," so, faced with the struggle and sacrifice of the daily lives, some women may even long for what they believe were simpler times.

Such nostalgia is misplaced. Women should keep moving forward, perfecting our inherent qualities of cooperation, collaboration, compassion, inclusion, loyalty, and social justice—the same qualities required for the formation of democratic societies. Indeed, women deserve to be more than the subjects of laws and the targets of marketing strategies. We should own shops, sit on boards, function as CEOs and presidents, and, at the very least, participate in developing economic policies designed to help us. If we women fail to support each other, choosing instead to retreat from the battle for our own emancipation, everything we have accomplished will fall into decay, and then, as we say in Arabic, "Only our own eyes will weep for us."

Saved by Love

ALS IS PROBABLY APPARENT, MY COUNTRY'S WOMEN'S MOVE-
ment is a subject that I care about quite passionately. Telling my first
group of American students about Egypt's feminists, my heroines
and role models, made being alone in America seem a little less
stressful and a lot more promising. At first, I read my lectures word
for word. I was too insecure to relax and improvise or rely on my
own abilities to relay to others what I knew so well. Standing
behind a podium, my eyes glued to a script lest I lose my place, I
can only imagine that I was a spectacularly boring speaker. The
boredom, I hope, was somewhat relieved when I concluded my
formal presentation to take questions from the students. To my surprise, none were related to my lecture. The students wanted to
know more about me than they did about Egypt's feminist pioneers. If I had known this ahead of time, perhaps I would not have
worked so long and hard to prepare myself. To my students, I was
a curiosity, an Arab woman they might come to understand. They

asked about my life with Anwar Sadat, my children, Cairo, my grandchildren, and even my hobbies. Their obvious interest and warm welcome helped put me at ease, so that eventually I could stop reading my lessons and refer instead to my notes to cue me when I digressed. Later, I even dared impromptu lecturing, though I kept the typed script clutched firmly in my hand in case I faltered. In South Carolina, I began the process of mastering my own thoughts.

Learning how to stand on my own was not easy. Part of me hated the thought of shedding the Sadat mantle. As comforting as it was to take refuge in memories of our life together, our partnership in service of our country, Anwar was gone. I could not depend on him to draft my lectures, teach my classes, or pay my bills. In those early years in America, I was desperate to find instructions on how to be a widow. I began reading autobiographies and biographies as if they were how-to manuals. I thought that if I understood the happiness and hardship of women like Eleanor Roosevelt and Jacqueline Kennedy, I could better cope with my own situation. Although their experiences and decisions were quite different from mine, I was convinced their stories could strengthen both my desire and my ability to be independent. They would teach me how to live on my own in the United States. I also read and reread Virginia Woolf's celebrated essay *A Room of One's Own*, which buoyed me intellectually. In it, Woolf argues that in order for a woman to create, she must have a roof over her head and a space she can call her own. Even though she was describing a woman's place within the art world, her thesis is applicable to every facet of a woman's life. I am living proof that Virginia Woolf's words are as true today as they were when they were written: a woman needs a room of her own—or, better yet, a house.

For the first time in my life, I own my home, which I bought and paid for with money I earned. Contrary to some people's assumptions, Anwar and I did not have palatial properties all over the world. Even my house in Giza is the property of the Egyptian government, leased to me for my lifetime. But my home in Virginia is all mine. It is by no means a mansion, but it is spacious and comfortable and imparts the flavor of the Middle East in a Washington suburb. In Egypt, I will always be the president's wife, revered and surrounded by people eager to do everything for me. In America, for the first time in my adult life, I could venture out in public on my own. I took inordinate pleasure in my trips to the grocery store, where I could wander the aisles, free to follow the grocery lists that I had drawn up or load my cart with impulse buys.

Although I had been working outside my home for many years in Egypt, here in this new milieu, everything was different: I did not know about working in America or presenting myself as an independent woman. Furthermore, in Egypt I had never received a salary, except a small one from my teaching position at Cairo University, which I donated to the university's custodial staff, whose salaries were a pittance—members of what Americans call the *working poor*. Thus, when I received my first paycheck, I was confused. I held it, inspected it, turned it over and over in my hand, staring at my name printed in bold black letters, all the while wondering what to do with such a large sum of money.

When I was growing up in Egypt, no one used banks and checks. Private and public sector employers paid their employees in cash. On the first day of each month, public employees waited in a long queue in front of the Department of Finance in order to receive their salaries. Of course, it is not that way today. Pensions, a social security program initiated by my husband, are now automatically forwarded to a bank account for those who have them. More modern-minded Egyptians rely on credit cards, and there are

ATMs in all of our tourist spots. Many Egyptians, however, especially those in rural areas who are not ready to let go of old habits, still deal only in cash. I am not surprised when I occasionally see my countrymen with pockets stuffed with wrinkled bills. In the past, it was not unusual for Egyptians to hoard all their money under the mattress, *taht al-balata,* or beneath the floor tiles in their homes, so they could be sure they could get to it whenever they needed it. Here in the States, I laugh every time I read about some eccentric old penny-pincher who has stashed stacks of cash under the mattress or in cookie jars. "Oh," I think, "this is not an American. This is an Egyptian."

In the case of my paycheck, however, I neither wanted to hide my money nor save it all. I wanted to spend it on gifts for my children and grandchildren. After a couple of days, I said, "You are a crazy girl, Jehan. Just ask your neighbor for the name of her bank." And I did. The very next day, brimming with confidence and my kind neighbor's instructions, armed with my identity card, social security card, green card, and passport, I arrived at the bank ready and eager to open my first bank account. Something so ordinary to the majority of Americans was a watershed moment for me. It tangibly symbolized the starting point of my new life. I was no longer merely Jehan Sadat, widow of Egypt's slain president, Anwar Sadat. I had been transformed into an independent, modern woman, working and living on my own. I was torn, as I so often am, between feelings of happiness and sorrow—nostalgia for the past and anticipation of the future.

That future came calling a few years later when two Middle Eastern professors at the University of South Carolina contacted me. They wanted me to know how much they appreciated what my husband had done and had sacrificed for peace in our part of the world. They also wanted to tell me about a lovely and ambitious idea: the establishment of a memorial to President Sadat in the United States, a living monument that would perpetuate his legacy and promote world peace. In the past, others had approached me with similar ideas, but nothing had ever materialized. Although I cautioned myself against getting too excited, I was nevertheless encouraged by their enthusiasm.

Not long after our conversation, I learned from a colleague that they had transferred to the University of Maryland, College Park. The next I heard from them was an invitation to join them in their "Sadat project." I could hardly believe the progress they had made since our conversation. Their goal was the creation of a scholarly chair at the university. By 1988, their dream, the Anwar Sadat Chair for Population, Development, and Peace, now called the Anwar Sadat Chair for Development and Peace, was taking shape within the Center for International Development and Conflict Management at the University of Maryland. That was enough to convince me to join them, albeit only for a year, for I still planned to return to Egypt. God, however, had other plans, and that one-year commitment grew into a career that has completely changed my life.

Our first step was to organize an advisory committee. We determined that I should set out on what would prove to be a long and arduous schedule of fund-raising appearances. We needed $1.5 million to endow the Anwar Sadat Chair, so I went anywhere people would have me. For several years, most of the honoraria and monetary awards given me went to the chair. Anyone willing to stage an event to benefit the Anwar Sadat Chair could count on my being the first one there. I did not care if I would be talking with a small group gathered in someone's living room or to thousands in a huge auditorium. Flying throughout the United States and Canada, traveling far from Washington to Russia, Taiwan, England, France, Germany, South Korea, Brazil, and places in between was hectic but infinitely rewarding. I was speaking about my husband's efforts for peace, the future of the Middle East, and women's equality. I was pushing myself to get beyond the fatigue and jet lag. I felt that I was being tested emotionally, intellectually, and physically, and I would not be found wanting.

Exhausting as the pace could be, my travels marked a new phase in my education. I met and spoke with many people who challenged, refined, and deepened my commitment to peace. In addition, I found I had genuinely come to love public speaking. After my husband's death, I forced myself to accept the invitations I received to address foreign organizations and universities. These occasions were brief glimmers of light in an otherwise dark time. As the number of requests increased, I started thinking that perhaps public speaking would be a good way for me to earn my living without being saddled with long-term commitments, of which I was wary. The idea of talking freely and openly about issues that were important to me was an attractive offer, but it was also profoundly depressing. Each time I thought about Anwar in the past tense, I wept. Still, it was appealing to me, because for so long, I had trained myself to be cautious about everything I said and did. When I was first lady, my every action was dissected, analyzed, and scrutinized. Living in such a fishbowl was mentally, physically, and emotionally exhausting. I feared that in voicing my opinions, I would make some verbal misstep that would bring criticism to Anwar. And often it did. As much as I reminded myself that discretion is the better part of valor, I have always felt an obligation to say what I believe to be right—even when doing so had the potential of causing problems for my husband. Throughout my public life, I had longed for the time when no one would tell me that what I was saying was either wrong or right. By the time I was traveling on behalf of the Sadat Chair, I knew that a career in public speaking was my open stage, a place where I could present my ideas and make public my convictions without grave political repercussions. Most important, it would give me the perfect opportunity to keep my husband's memory alive. And it seems I have a lot left to say.

The breakneck schedule nevertheless had wonderful moments. I remember in particular, one benefit in Los Angeles, where President and Mrs. Reagan were special attendees. Anwar and I had come to know them during an official visit to the United States during that terrible summer of 1981, just a short time before Anwar was killed, when sectarian violence erupted in Egypt and the peace process was under siege. Later I felt a particular bond with Nancy. She loved her husband so much: to watch him succumb day by day to Alzheimer's must have been terrible. Speaking as a person who lost her mother, brother, and sister to that dreadful disease, I know firsthand the pain of watching a loved one slowly vanish. Nancy Reagan once said that not being able to share the memories was the hardest part of her husband's disease. I understand. When I was first lady, there were few things I looked forward to so much as the day when Anwar and I could, from the blessed calm of our retirement, look back on the tumultuous events of our lives. Part of me shall always mourn the future we never shared.

On that day in California, however, President Reagan was every bit the "Great Communicator." True to form, he summed up the goal of the Sadat Chair beautifully: "The establishment of the Anwar Sadat Chair for Population, Development and Peace was a bold move much like President Sadat's visit to Jerusalem in 1977. We must keep that drive, that dedication for the peaceful resolution of conflict alive in the hearts of the world leaders everywhere. The Sadat Chair will bring together political and academic leaders to explore new ways to peacefully resolve conflicts of our world.

It is a bold step, a new way to look at age-old problems that cause so much pain and suffering."

Finally, on October 7, 1997, President Ezer Weizman of Israel presented the first Sadat Lecture for Peace at the investiture of the Sadat Chair. My dream had come true, and I could think of no more fitting person than President Weizman to preside over this joyous occasion—not only for the friendship he and my husband had shared, but also because these two extraordinary men had first known one another across a field of battle. President Weizman was commander of the Israeli Air Force and played a significant role in the Arab defeat in the 1967 war. Later, this former hawk came to realize that peace with Egypt was in his country's best interests. And so it was at the Camp David meetings that Anwar Sadat and Ezer Weizman recognized in one another a kindred spirit, and despite decades of enmity between their two countries, they came to love each other as brothers. Their friendship personifies hope for the Middle East and provides proof that peace is the triumph of love over hate. For many years, President Weizman and his wife, Reuma, called me on October 6 in remembrance of my husband. Now that she is also a widow, Reuma makes the call alone.

The chair was in place. I could scarcely believe it—nor did I have much time to reflect on it, for then the work began (though if what I had been doing before was merely the warm-up, I couldn't imagine what the "real" work might be!). One of our first projects was a colloquium between the students of Bir Zeit University in Palestine and Hebrew University in Jerusalem. Never before had Arab and Israeli students of these two institutions been given an opportunity to sit together to discuss the future of the peoples of their region. The Sadat Chair proudly sponsors events like this in order to promote the mutual dialogue of peace that is essential to understanding in the Middle East and throughout the rest of the world. The Anwar Sadat Chair aspires to narrow the gap between the world of academia and the world of policymakers, spheres that I know from experience often seem light-years apart, by enhancing the availability of the latest research to the international governmental community that, for us, is located only a few miles away in Washington. We are also reaching out to the youth of Maryland with an essay competition: the Sadat Essay for Peace encourages young people to think about issues related to world peace and to contemplate the impact that President Sadat's legacy of working toward peace has had on those issues. The chair also invites internationally known leaders to deliver the annual Sadat Lecture. The second lecture, held in October 1998, marked the twentieth anniversary of the Camp David Peace Accords, so of course it featured former president and noble statesman, and my dear friend, the Honorable Jimmy Carter. Former U.S. Secretary of State Henry Kissinger has also delivered a Sadat lecture, as have former UN Secretary General Kofi Annan, former president Nelson Mandela of South Africa, former U.S. Secretary of State James Baker III, International Atomic Energy Agency director General Mohamed El Baradei, U.S. Senator George Mitchell, and former president Mary Robinson of Ireland.

These days, although I am a tenured professor at the University of Maryland, I do not teach regularly scheduled classes. Like many others in my position, I teach special sessions and give lectures to new faculty members, renowned scholars on staff, and retired professors who remain involved with the academic community. I hold positions on various committees, confer with the staff at the Center for International Development and Conflict Management where the Sadat Chair is housed, and meet with students, staff, and distinguished guests at the university. I also serve on and lend my name to advisory boards for numerous charity and artistic groups. In Cairo, I speak to many groups and host alumni and faculty of the University of Maryland in my home, as well as dignitaries from all over the world. I truly enjoy the relationship I have with the University of Maryland. All the activities in which I am involved are intellectually stimulating and afford me opportunities to exchange ideas with my colleagues, noteworthy guests, and young people. And so my education and journey through life continue.

Not too long ago I was honored to receive the Anne Morrow Lindbergh Award for Aging with Grace and Distinction at the Baylor College of Medicine in Houston. I was delighted when I received the letter of invitation, because I am not only fond of Texas and glad for any excuse to get there, but the subject of the conference, women's health, is important to me. In Egypt I have long advocated programs that educate women about threats to their health and encourage them to seek early and proper medical attention. Finally, I was glad of this particular invitation because there is a quote from Anne Morrow Lindbergh that I have had ample opportunity to reflect on, something that speaks very much to the experience of the Middle East: She said, "I do not believe that sheer suffering teaches. If suffering alone taught, the entire world would be wise, since everyone suffers. To suffering must be added mourning, understanding, patience, love, openness, and the willingness to remain vulnerable."

Indeed, I was feeling quite pleased until I reread the title of the award that Baylor proposed to grant me: Aging with Grace and Distinction. "Wait just a minute," I thought. "Are they trying to tell me I'm old?"

Frankly, I do not give too much thought to my age. I am healthy and active. I have my family and my friends. I go out. I fly back and forth between Washington and Cairo several times a year. Naguib Mahfouz, Egypt's Nobel laureate in literature and one of my favorite writers, wrote in his *Echoes of an Autobiography*: "Some people are preoccupied with life; others are preoccupied with death. As for me, my position is firmly in the middle way." Age, like time, holds little meaning to most Egyptians. In Islam, we say, "Work for the world as though you will live forever and prepare for the hereafter as though you will die tomorrow." Both of these statements reflect perfectly my attitude toward life.

A colleague once asked, "Mrs. Sadat, why do you continue working? The Sadat Chair is in place now. I would think you would want to rest after all these years." Rest does sound inviting. Rest means I would have more time with my family, which, in addition to my four children and their spouses, encompasses eleven grandchildren and eight great-grandchildren. But rest is not for me. I am not ready to retire. The Sadat Chair has been established, but comprehensive peace in the Middle East has yet to be achieved.

My husband reached the peak of his worldly achievements when he brought peace to Egypt. When I lost him, my bereavement nearly robbed me of my hope and shook the foundation of my faith. I shut myself away, drained of my usual enthusiasm, yet with prayer and the support of my family, I rediscovered myself— and my mission: to continue the message of peace for which my husband had lost his life. Anwar is physically absent—nothing more. For years, I have been doing my best to perpetuate the legacy of Anwar Sadat, spreading his message and mine that peace between Arabs and Israelis is possible and so, too, peace between Islam—the faith that sustains and defines me—and the West; peace between ordinary individuals who have forgotten, as we all sometimes do, that others who appear, or speak, or pray differently nevertheless share our common humanity. After so many years, I think

I can call myself a peacemaker in my own right. Indeed, I love my job, and there's no denying that it is a steady one. I have always said that those working for peace and harmony in the world will never be unemployed.

Is peace attainable? I believe it is. Is it something I will live to see? In this instance, I shall let Reinhold Niebuhr, the Protestant theologian and champion of social justice, answer for me: "Nothing worth doing is completed in our lifetime; therefore, we are saved by hope. Nothing true or beautiful or good makes complete sense in any immediate context of history; therefore, we are saved by faith. Nothing we do, however virtuous, can be accomplished alone; therefore, we are saved by love."

Afterword

S OME YEARS AGO, A CLOSE FRIEND, A HIGHLY ACCOMPLISHED, independent, professional woman in her forties, converted to Islam. I was surprised; she is American, brought up in the Baptist Church, and although a significant number of American women are converting to Islam (exact numbers are hard to come by), I had not encountered very many. Moreover, in these days in which being a Muslim is often believed to be incompatible with being a patriot (that Barack Obama was "smeared" by allegations he was a Muslim spoke volumes), I did not imagine that the path of the Muslim convert in the United States is an easy one. I could not help worrying that I had somehow influenced her choice. I quizzed her again and again on her decision: Why had she left behind her own tradition? What did her family think?

In the many conversations we had on the subject, she answered my questions patiently. "Jehan," she explained, "for me Islam represents all that is beautiful in the world's three monotheistic religions. As I was reading, I found so many references, positive ones, in the Qur'an to people of faith, Christians and Jews as well as Muslims. For me, Islam, in a very profound way, is the best of all three religions."

She spoke with clarity and passion, but still I wondered. Her decision had come at some personal cost. Her father accepted her choice without reservation, but her mother was angry and distraught. She could not understand why her only child had joined a "religion of radical fundamentalists." Obviously I disagreed with her mother's mistaken views of Islam, but more important than that, I identified with her concern for her daughter.

One day my friend came to my house for lunch. When it was time for *zuhur,* the midday prayer, I asked if she would prefer to pray alone or to join me. She said she would join me. We spread the prayer rugs in the direction of the Kaa'ba, silently covered our hair and removed our shoes. As I began to recite the incomparable words of the Holy Qur'an, I saw that my friend had indeed learned to pray as a Muslim. As we moved in quiet synchrony, my anxiety that I had somehow influenced my friend toward this choice vanished. I realized that her relationship with God was her own. She was called to Islam not by anything I said or did, but rather by a greater power.

I relate this story for two reasons. First, it demonstrates something I know to be true about Islam: it is a faith for today, one that a strong, independent, successful "career woman" can embrace without reservation. Second, it reminded me that God speaks to us on a level that is deeper than culture or ethnicity. Indeed, God speaks to our hearts. It did not matter that Islam might seem foreign to my friend's family and neighbors. She had found a spiritual home.

I did, however, continue to urge her to reconcile with her

mother. I told her that she must go to her, endeavor to please her in whatever way she could, because God does not want us to hurt our mothers, not ever. After all, paradise lies at the feet of mothers. Eventually, after much encouragement on my part and polite stubbornness on hers, she relented. One day she called me. "Jehan, I did it. I did what you said. But I have to admit that I didn't think you were right. No way. At first, when I was listening to you, I was listening only with my head, and I knew you were wrong. I knew you didn't really understand. Then I decided to listen to you with my heart, and when I started doing that, it no longer seemed so impossible to go to my mother, to talk to her. You were right."

Of course, it wasn't *me* who was right. It was her willingness to open her heart, her mind, to forgive, to try again in the face of what she imagined would be a painful repudiation. I know how difficult it is to allow our hearts to guide us. But I am convinced that it is on this path all our hopes depend, on a personal and a political level. I understand the wages of war and the cost of peace.

Peace, not only the peace between nations or quarreling parties but also the sense of peace that seeks a permanent home in our hearts and souls, is a conscious decision, a mindful, deliberate act. Peace is recognition of our mutual imperfections. Peace is our awareness and appreciation of each other and our shared need for human contact. Peace is not a complicated concept reserved for theologians, scholars, philosophers, and politicians to understand or achieve for us, but something we are called to as humans.

Peace is something we can build.

I have titled this book *My Hope for Peace*. Perhaps it should have been titled *My Hopes*—for indeed, they are many, and specific.

As the new presidential administration settles in, it is imperative that the U.S. government realize that peace between Arabs and Israelis must again be a foreign policy priority—that our fight against global terrorism will be conceived as a multinational, multifaith effort, and that Muslims will be regarded as allies, not adversaries. I hope that the interfaith conversation will continue and grow more robust. I hope that the world will cease to distinguish between Muslims and what publications by organizations ranging from the Pew Charitable Trusts to *Foreign Affairs* persist in calling their "host" countries, implying that we are guests rather than engaged citizens. I hope that Muslims will make an effort to reach out, to counter challenges within and outside our community, and demonstrate the principles—brotherhood, justice, charity, peace—by which this religion is great. I hope people will suspend, every so often, a bit of the cynicism, a bit of the certitude, that the Middle East can only be convulsed by bloody conflagration. Peace is possible. The world witnessed a breakthrough in 1979, and it can happen again.

In April 2008, President Jimmy Carter made a trip to the Middle East in an effort to shore up the faltering post-Annapolis peace process. The Annapolis Conference, which was hosted by President George W. Bush and Secretary of State Condoleezza Rice at the U.S. Naval Academy in Annapolis, Maryland, in November 2007, had brought together Ehud Olmert and Mahmoud Abbas, as well as envoys from some fifty nations, including sixteen from the Arab League, to discuss a path forward toward a two-state solution—a goal that was, for the first time, formally articulated by the Israelis as well as the Palestinians. Although this alone was a milestone and plans were made for further talks, the months that followed saw few changes on the ground: Israel did not halt settlement activity, the situation caused by Israeli military checkpoints was not significantly altered, and Abbas could not bring more radical Palestinian factions to heel. Indeed, Hamas had been entirely excluded from the talks. Thus, when Jimmy Carter traveled to the Middle East in

April 2008, he hoped to reinvigorate the process by opening lines of communication. He met with Hamas leaders and Syrian president Bashir Assad. His decision to meet with what the United States deems "pariahs" was controversial and brought sharp condemnation from many quarters. I fear, however, that President Carter's critics are afflicted with a "can't-do" attitude that traps us all in a horrific quagmire of conflict and mistrust.

My husband believed that peace demands that we talk with our enemies. How else do we resolve differences? It is obvious that isolating and ignoring Hamas, the leadership elected by the Palestinian people but classified as a terrorist group by the United States, is not working, is not putting an end to the decades-old conflict. Moreover, it seems that Syria is ready and willing to enter into a comprehensive peace with Israel. I am not surprised that Carter, who, along with Sadat and Begin, broke so many barriers, would exemplify the kind of daring that is called for to open meaningful channels of communication among all the parties. Common sense requires us to acknowledge that anything less than multilateral talks makes a lasting peace all but impossible. Sadly, it seems that common sense is in short supply. President Carter can act with comparative freedom, because he is involved in a nongovernmental organization, the Carter Center, and no longer holds public office. Furthermore, no other American president has his expertise and experience in Mideast affairs. In the presidential race, Then-Senator Barack Obama was severely criticized for stating that he would not oppose opening discussions with Iran and Syria. What's wrong with this thinking?

Indeed, in the United States and in the Middle East, people want peace. Is it really so difficult to understand that whether American or Iraqi, Palestinian or Israeli, we all want our sons and daughters to stop dying, to live in peace? Is it really so difficult to understand that finding an end to the bloodshed requires, in every case, hard work, compromise, and a willingness to realize that great wrongs have been committed on all sides?

I will perhaps be accused by some pundits of oversimplifying, of paying insufficient attention to the subtleties and complications (the history! the hatred! the military and economic ramifications!) that preclude simple solutions. Yet more than thirty years ago, my husband made a difficult but simple choice: to make peace his political and personal priority. And despite the subtleties and complications (the history! the hatred! the military and economic ramifications!), he gave us a peace that has endured. The same can happen today. We must make a choice between our desire to prevail, to punish, and to avenge past generations—whose sufferings I neither belittle nor brush aside—and the generations to come, who might, with our help, slowly free themselves of the snares of history.

I will always hope for peace. I will always pray for peace. And so I say to you, *As-salaam aleikum*, Peace be upon you.

Bibliography

Abou El Fadl, Khaled. *And God Knows the Soldiers: The Authoritative and Authoritarian in Islamic Discourses.* Lanham, Md.: University Press of America, 2001.

———. "Islam and the Challenge of Democracy." *Boston Review,* May 2003.

Ahmed, Akbar S. *Islam Today. A Short Introduction.* London: IB Tauris, 1999.

The Amman Message. http://ammanmessage.com/.

Armstrong, Karen. *A History of Jerusalem: One City, Three Faiths.* New York: Harper Perennial, 1996.

———. *Islam: A Short History.* New York: Modern Library, 2002.

Asani, Ali S. "On Pluralism, Tolerance and the Qu'ran." *American Scholar* 71 (winter 2002): 52–60.

Aslan, Reza. *No God But God: The Origins, Evolution, and Future of Islam.* New York: Random House, 2005.

Badran, Margot. *Feminists, Islam and Nation: Gender and the Making of Modern Egypt.* Princeton: Princeton University Press, 2001.

Carter, Jimmy. *The Blood of Abraham.* Boston: Houghton Mifflin, 1985.

———. *Palestine, Peace Not Apartheid.* New York: Simon & Schuster, 2006.

Cohen, Roger. "Her Jewish State." *New York Times Magazine,* July 8, 2007.

Council on American Islamic Relations. *American Public Opinion About Islam and Muslims*. 2006. www.cair.com/cairsurveyanalysis.pdf-2006-12-18.

Council on American Islamic Relations. *American Muslim Voters, A Demographic Profile and a Survey of Attitudes*. October 24, 2006. www.cair.com/annreport/AmericanMuslimVoters.pdf.

Dean, Claudia, and Darryl Fears. "Negative Perception of Islam Increasing: Poll Numbers in United States Higher Than in 2001." *Washington Post,* March 9, 2006.

Dowd, Maureen. "Liberties: Cleopatra and Osama." *New York Times,* November 18, 2001.

El-Ahwal, Abdelkarim. "A Socio-Cultural Account of the Sadat Peace Initiative." *Proceedings from the PWPA Colloquium on the Sadat Peace Initiative: A Scholarly Appraisal Ten Years Later*. New York: Professors of World Peace Academy Press, 1989.

Esposito, John. *Political Islam: Revolution, Radicalism, or Reform*. Cairo: American University in Cairo Press, 1997.

Esposito, John, and Dalia Mogahed. *Who Speaks for Islam? What a Billion Muslims Really Think*. New York: Gallup Press, 2008.

Fay, Mary Ann. "International Feminism and the Women's Movement in Egypt, 1904–1923." Presented at the Conference on Institutions, Ideologies and Agencies, Changing Family Life in the Arab Middle East, University of North Carolina at Chapel Hill, April 2003.

Goldschmidt, Arthur. *A Concise History of the Middle East*. Cairo: American University in Cairo Press, 2002.

Gorenberg, Gershom. *The Accidental Empire: Israel and the Birth of the Settlements, 1967–1977*. New York: Holt, 2006.

Ibrahim, Saad Eddin. *Egypt, Islam and Democracy: Critical Essays*. Cairo: American University in Cairo Press, 2002.

Kissinger, Henry. *Years of Upheaval*. New York: Little, Brown, 1982.

Kutzer, Daniel, and Scott B. Lasensky. *Negotiating Arab Israeli Peace: American Leadership in the Middle East*. Washington, D.C.: United States Institute of Peace Press, 2008.

Lindbergh, Anne Morrow. *Hour of Gold, Hour of Lead: Diaries and Letters of Anne Morrow Lindbergh*. New York: Harvest, 1973.

Livani, Talajeh. "Middle East and North Africa: Gender Overview." The

World Bank, 2007. http://siteresources.worldbank.org/INTMENA/Resources/MENA_Gender_Overview_2007.pdf.

———. "What We've Learned About Suicide Terrorism Since 9/11." *Chicago Tribune*, September 11, 2006.

Mahfouz, Naguib. *Echoes of an Autobiography*. Cairo: American University in Cairo Press, 1997.

Pape, Robert. *Dying to Win: The Strategic Logic of Suicide Terrorism*. New York: Random House, 2006.

Pew Forum on Religion and Public Life. "Public Expresses Mixed Views of Islam, Mormonism." September 25, 2007. http://pewforum.org/surveys/religionviews07.pdf.

Qutb, Sayyed. *Milestones*. India: Islamic Book Service India, 2006.

Rauf, Imam Feisal Abdul. *What's Right with Islam*. San Francisco: HarperSanFrancisco, 2004.

Rauf, Mohammed Abdul. *The Islamic View of Women and the Family*. New York: Robert Speller & Sons, 1977.

Ross, Dennis. *The Missing Peace*. New York: Farrar, Straus and Giroux, 2004.

Roudi-Fahimi, Farzaneh, and Valentine M. Moghadam. *Empowering Women, Developing Society: Female Education in the Middle East and North Africa*. Population Reference Bureau Report. 2008. http://www.prb.org/pdf/EmpoweringWomeninMENA.pdf.

Sadat, Anwar. *In Search of an Identity*. New York: Harper, 1977.

———. *Those I Have Known*. New York: Continuum, 1984.

Sadat, Jehan. *A Woman of Egypt*. New York: Simon & Schuster, 1987.

Sedgwick, Mark. *Sufism: The Essentials*. Cairo: American University in Cairo Press, 2000.

Sommers, Christina Hoff. "The Subjection of Women in the Islamic World." *Weekly Standard*, May 21, 2007.

Stein, Jeff. "Can You Tell a Sunni from a Shiite?" *New York Times*, October 17, 2006.

Stein, Kenneth. "Sadat, Carter and Begin, an Unequally Sided Triangle." In *The Camp David Process*. Jerusalem: Menachem Begin Heritage Centre, 2002.

Telhami, Shibley. *2008 Annual Arab Public Opinion Poll: Survey of the Anwar Sadat Chair for Peace and Development at the University of Maryland with Zogby International*. February 2008. http://www.brookings.edu/

topics/2008/~/media/Files/events/2008/0414_middle_east/0414_mid
dle_east_telhami.pdf.

United Nations. *The Humanitarian Impact of the West Bank Barrier on Pales-tinian Communities.* New York: United Nations, March 2005.

United Nations Development Programme. *World Population Prospects 1950–2050: 2007/2008 Report, Demographic Trends.* New York: United Nations, July 2007.

United Nations Information System on the Question of Palestine. *The Origins and Evolution of the Palestine Problem: 1917–1988. Part II: 1947–1977.* June 30, 1990.

United Nations Relief and Works Agency for Palestine Refugees in the Near East. "History and Establishment of UNRWA." http://www.un.org/unrwa/overview/qa.html.

Wolfe, Michael, ed. *Taking Back Islam: American Muslims Reclaim Their Faith.* New York: Rodale Press, 2002.

Wright, Lawrence. *The Looming Tower: Al-Qaeda and the Road to 9/11.* New York: Knopf, 2006.

Zogby International. "Report Card on American Prejudice," July 2007. http://www.zogby.com/gsn/GSNReport.pdf.

Jehan Sadat, Ph.D.

Awards and Honors

Volunteer of the Year, presented by Rehabilitation International United States

Paul Harris Fellow, presented by the Rotary Foundation of Rotary International

Commissioner's Award, presented by Rehabilitation Services Administration, United States Department of Health, Education, and Welfare

Grand Cross of Merit, presented by the Italian Red Cross

Distinguished Public Service Award, presented by United States Department of Health and Human Services

Margaret Sanger Award, presented by Planned Parenthood Federation of America

Living Legacy Award, presented by Women's International Center, WIC Honorary President since 1984

International Humanitarian Award, first recipient, presented by Crittenton Center

Distinguished Professor Award, first recipient, presented by Radford University

International Humanitarian Award for Global Dedication to Women's and Children's Causes, Los Angeles, California

International Children's Peace Prize, presented by Disneyland, Anaheim, California

Achievement Award, presented by Baylor University, Waco, Texas

Eleanor Roosevelt Award, presented by the United Nations, San Francisco

Children's Champion, presented by the Washington UNICEF Council

International Award, presented in São Paulo, Brazil
Woman of Achievement Award, presented by Zonta International
The Love, Dignity, Honor, Peace Award, presented by the Center for
    Human Nutrition, Omaha, Nebraska
Chairman's Award, in recognition of lifelong contribution to global under-
    standing, presented by Memphis Symphony Balls
Women of Distinction Award, Little Rock, Arkansas
Tribute to Three Women of the Middle East: Farah Pahlavi, Leah Rabin, and
    Jehan Sadat, Friends of Tel Aviv University, Washington, D.C.
The Eloise ReQua International Humanitarian Award, Library of Interna-
    tional Relations, Chicago
Network 2000: Women of Excellence, Baltimore, Maryland

Honorary Doctorates

Philippine Women's University, Manila, Philippines
DePaul University, Chicago, Illinois
University of South Carolina, Columbia, South Carolina
New York University, New York, New York
Vermont University, Burlington, Vermont
Hamline University, St. Paul, Minnesota
Wheaton College, Norton, Massachusetts
University of Nevada, Las Vegas, Nevada
American University, Washington, D.C.
Saint John's University, Collegeville, Minnesota
Hofstra University, Hempstead, New York
Dowling College, Oakdale, New York
Rochester Institute of Technology, Rochester, New York
University of Health Sciences, Kansas City, Missouri
University of Maryland, College Park, Maryland
Brigham Young University, Provo, Utah
Miami University, Oxford, Ohio
Simmons School of Leadership, Boston, Massachusetts
University of Central Florida, Orlando, Florida
The Pennsylvania State University, University Park, Pennsylvania

CONFERENCES

United Nations International Women's Conference, Mexico City, Mexico
International Parliamentary Conference on Population and Development, Sri Lanka
World Conference of the United Nations Decade for Women, Copenhagen, Denmark
Governor's Women's Conference, Las Vegas, Nevada
United Nations International Year of the Family Conference, Minneapolis, Minnesota
People to People International, Newport Beach, California
State of the World Forum, San Francisco, California
Insights 96, San Diego, California
International Women's Forum, IBM and Center for International Private Enterprise, Washington, D.C.
State of the World Forum, Guanajuato, Mexico
Franklin Covey International Leadership Symposium, Salt Lake City, Utah
World Congress of Families II, Geneva, Switzerland
Accenture: Women in Government Leadership Conferences, San Francisco, New York, and Washington, D.C.
Phi Theta Kappa: International Conference, Nashville, Tennessee
International Peace Conference, Bochun, Germany
American Association of Community Colleges, Philadelphia, Pennsylvania
ATLAS Program, St. Louis University, Missouri
East Bay Women's Conference, Walnut Creek, California

Index

Index

National security issues, 21–22
Nawar, Abdel-Aziz, 89
Netanyahu, Benjamin, 100–101
Newark, New Jersey, riots in, 26
Niebuhr, Reinhold, 184
9/11 terrorist attacks, 3, 7–10,
    19–20, 35, 105
Nixon, Richard M., 79
Niyya (intention of believer), 5, 33
Nobel Peace Prize
    of 1979, 18, 87
    of 1994, 100
Norman and Florence Brody Family
    Public Policy Forum, Two
    Women of Peace: A
    Conversation with Leah Rabin
    and Jehan Sadat, 100
Northern Ireland, 114

Obama, Barack, 185, 189
Olmert, Ehud, 103, 104, 107, 188
Orabi Pasha, 122
*Origins and Evolution of the Palestine
    Problem, The* (United Nations),
    74
Oslo Accords, 95, 100–101
Oslo Declaration of Principles, 93,
    97
Ottoman Empire, 47, 64

Pahlavi, Farah Diba, 100
Pakistan, 37, 44, 63, 72
Palestine. *See also* Israel; Palestinians
    British and, 64–66, 68
    Jewish immigrants to, 65–66
    partition plan of 1947, 66–68
Palestine, Peace Not Apartheid (Carter),
    64

Palestine Liberation Organization
    (PLO)
    Camp David talks of 2000, 101
    charter of, 76
    creation of, 73
    in Lebanon, 78, 92
    Oslo Accords and, 95
Palestinian National Authority, 93
    creation of, 95
Palestinians, 18, 43, 44, 62, 63
    Gulf War of 1991 and, 94
    Hamas and, 95–96, 104
    Israeli-Palestinian conflict, 76,
        83–85, 90–91, 95–97,
        100–114, 116, 120, 123, 188
    Jordan and, 76, 78
    in occupied territories, 74
    in refugee camps, 68, 69, 71, 74,
        75, 92, 110–111
Pan-Arab movement, 34, 75, 118
Pape, Robert, 43
Peace Now movement (Israel), 116
Pearl S. Buck Award, 22
Peres, Shimon, 100
Pew Forum on Religion and Public
    Life polls, 26–29
Pilgrimage (*hajj*), 32
Political Islam (Esposito), 45
Polygamy, 135, 146, 149–150
Popular Front for the Liberation of
    Palestine (PFLP), 82
Prayer (*salat*), 32
Predestination, 31
Preemption, doctrine of, 29–30

Qalamawi, Suheir, 163–164
Qalqilya, 102
Qatar, 93, 128

Index

Sahih el-Bukhari, 136
Salah el-Din, 112, 113
Salat (prayer), 32
Saudi Arabia, 37, 44, 57–58, 93
Saum (fasting), 32
Scowcroft, Brent, 105
Seljuks, 113
Sha'arawi, Huda, 158–160, 162, 164
Shahada (declaration of faith), 32
Sharia law, 20, 46, 48, 145, 150
Sharon, Ariel, 92, 101, 103, 107
Sheikhs and imams, role of, 34–35
Shiite Islam, 35–37
Sinai, 17, 18, 50, 72–74, 75, 80, 86, 109
Six-Day War of 1967, 16–17, 61, 73–75, 80, 107, 109, 122, 180
"Socio-Cultural Account of the Sadat Peace Initiative, A" (El-Ahwal), 90
Sommers, Christina Hoff, 129–130
SOS Children's Village, 91, 153
South Yemen, 82
Soviet Jews, 109
Soviet Union, Egypt and, 72, 73, 78–80, 118
Spain
    medieval, 46–47
    Muslim population in, 26
Sri Lanka, 43
State, U.S. Department of, 12, 73
Stein, Jeff, 35
Stern Gang, 66
Straits of Tiran, 73
"Subjection of Islamic Women, The" (Sommers), 129–130
Suez Canal, 14, 36, 71, 72, 74, 75, 80

Sufism, 38–39
Suicide bombings, 11, 42–43, 96, 100, 104–106
Sunna, 31
Sunni Islam, 11, 34–37, 136
Syria, 37, 64, 82, 129, 165
    Israel and, 73, 109, 189
    Palestinians and, 68, 91, 92, 111
    Six-Day War of 1967, 73, 109
    Yom Kippur War of 1973, 80

Taba talks, 113
Takfir (the act of declaring someone an apostate), 16, 39
Taliban, 129, 130
Talla Society cooperative, 91, 152–153
Tamil Tigers, 43
Tel Aviv, 81
Telkarum, 102
Tellawy, Mervat, 166
Temple Mount, Jerusalem, 101
Temple of Queen Hatshepsut, Luxor, Egypt, 12
"Three Nos," 75
Torah, 30
Transjordan, 64, 68
Trinity, the, 31
Tripoli, 92
Tunis, 78, 82, 92, 95
Tunisia, 93
Turkey, 38, 44, 72, 132
Tutu, Desmond, 104

United Arab Republic, 73
United Nations
    The Origins and Evolution of the Palestine Problem report, 74
    partition plan of 1947, 66–69

About the Author

Jehan Sadat is the author of the *New York Times* best-selling autobiography *A Woman of Egypt* and a Senior Fellow at the Anwar Sadat Chair for Peace and Development at the University of Maryland. She is the mother of four, grandmother of eleven, and great-grandmother of eight.

Printed in the United States
By Bookmasters